Voices of Hope

Voices of Hope

REDISCOVERING AND BUILDING HOPE FOR ALL

EDITED BY

JAN JORRIT HASSELAAR

MARK VAN VUUREN

JULIETA MATOS CASTAÑO

ERIK BORGMAN

Central European University Press

BUDAPEST–VIENNA–NEW YORK–AMSTERDAM

This book is partly made possible by 'Het Gerardusfonds' of the Roman Catholic Diocese of 's-Hertogenbosch, the Netherlands.

Voices of Hope is a collaboration between Vrije Universiteit Amsterdam (the Netherlands), University of the Free State (South Africa), and the Anglican Church of Southern Africa. The development of *Voices of Hope* began within the framework of the Jubilee Year 'Pilgrims of Hope', which was proclaimed by Pope Francis and later continued by Pope Leo XIV.

Cover design and lay-out: Margreet van de Burgt

ISBN 978 90 4857 734 7
E-ISBN 978 90 4857 793 4 (pdf)
E-ISBN 978 90 4857 794 1 (accessible ePub)
DOI 10.5117/9789048577347
NUR 728 | 740

CONTENTS

INTRODUCTION

Can we be surprised by hope once more in a world that seems so hopeless?

ABSTRACT

What do we actually mean when we speak of hope? This book returns to hope by drawing on intellectual, spiritual, and lived resources, bringing together essays about people from different backgrounds who have given voice to hope through reflection and action. Their lives and work ask us how to be inspired to rediscover and build hope in the world we inhabit today. This collection opens an ongoing inquiry, creating a shared reflective space where hope becomes something we can explore collectively.

KEYWORDS

hope, collective inquiry, voices of hope

The cultural critic Terry Eagleton noted in his book *Hope without Optimism* (2015) that hope had been a curiously neglected notion in a time marked by a growing sense that the future is slipping away from us. One decade later, the general impression is that the future is indeed slipping away. However, hope is no longer a neglected notion. On the contrary, the longing for hope seems to be everywhere, and we hear it invoked in politics, theology, education, activism, the arts,

Hasselaar, Jan Jorrit, Mark van Vuuren, Julieta Matos Castaño, and Erik Borgman, eds. *Voices of Hope: Rediscovering and Building Hope for All.* Amsterdam: Amsterdam University Press / Central European University Press, 2026.
 DOI 10.5117/9789048577347-1

and elsewhere. But the question remains urgent and unresolved: What do we actually mean when we speak of hope?

We are, of course, not the first to face despair in our times, just as we are not the first to ask questions about hope. Any attempt to answer such questions, therefore, should not start with us either. Humanity's intellectual and cultural heritage contains a vast and diverse reservoir of reflections on hope. Some reflections urge us to cling to hope, no matter the circumstances. Others claim that holding on to hope is difficult, maybe even too difficult. For some, hope feels naïve or even irresponsible in the face of today's challenges and the predicament of some groups of people. Others argue that hopelessness is the only honest position left, a way of acknowledging how dire our collective crises have become. Whether hope is possible or impossible, meaningful or naïve, absurd or necessary depends on what we understand hope to be. The bottom line remains that across centuries, (faith) traditions, and continents, people facing crisis, uncertainty, and transition have returned time and again to hope.

In this book, we also return to hope by tapping into deep resources. We have collected essays about people who have raised their voices about hope through reflection and action, through speaking and writing. Can they inspire us to rediscover and build hope in the world we inhabit today?

This collection invites readers into a process of reflection, opening up a shared space in which diverse understandings of hope can flourish rather than being fixed within a single framework. Approaching hope as a shared field of inquiry, we gathered together voices that reflect different (faith) traditions, disciplines, and lived experiences. These voices span different generations, genders, and geographical contexts – from the Global South to the Global North. Each entry also offers a list of references and bibliographical information selected by the experts who chose their particular voice of hope to be included in this volume.

Is it possible for us to be surprised by hope once more? This question runs through the contributions gathered here, which began to take shape in the context of a symposium called *Rediscover and Build Hope for All* held in Rome in June 2025. The symposium brought together initiatives from around the world, ranging from Pope Francis's and Pope Leo's 2025 Jubilee theme *Pilgrims of Hope* to the work of the Jonathan Sacks Institute, from Archbishop Thabo Makgoba's work on hope and reconciliation in South Africa to the academic focus on hope at the University of the Free State (South Africa), and the Vrije Universiteit Amsterdam's academic theme of the year in 2024–2025, *The Power of Hope*. The proceedings were kicked off by Archbishop Thabo Makgoba's reflections on hope and reconciliation in South Africa, based partly on lectures he had given earlier at the University of the Free State.

The symposium created a space for critical and respectful exchange, where scholars and practitioners from the Global South and Global North could seek a meaningful way forward together 'side by side', in the words of Chief Rabbi Jonathan Sacks.

This collection does not claim to offer the ultimate answer to the question of hope, nor does it present a single answer to what hope is or should be. Instead, we invite readers into an ongoing conversation in which hope is continually rediscovered and built anew in every time and context – a conversation to which we warmly welcome you.

Scan this QR code to get an impression of the symposium

Scan this QR code to join the Train of Hope, including some of the voices appearing in this publication

REFERENCES

Eagleton, T. (2015). *Hope without optimism.* University of Virginia Press.

ABOUT THE AUTHORS

Jan Jorrit Hasselaar, economist and theologian, is associate professor of public theology and director of the Amsterdam Centre for Religion & Sustainable Development at Vrije Universiteit Amsterdam, the Netherlands. He is a research fellow at the University of the Free State, South Africa. Jan Jorrit is co-chair of the Global Network for Public Theology.

Mark van Vuuren is associate professor of positive organizing at the University of Twente, the Netherlands.

Julieta Matos Castaño is a research associate at Vrije Universiteit Amsterdam and a practitioner in the field of futures thinking and design at Futures Compass, based in the Netherlands.

Erik Borgman is a lay Dominican and professor emeritus of public theology at Tilburg University, the Netherlands.

THOMAS AQUINAS

Hope means participation in God's love

BY ERIK BORGMAN

ARTWORK BY JANWILLEM HOFTIJZER

ABSTRACT

This essay elaborates on Thomas Aquinas's definition of hope as a virtue that orients us toward a difficult but attainable future good. As a virtue, hope guides individuals and communities to pursue transformation with the confidence that the future remains open to grace and the promise of ultimate fulfilment.

KEYWORDS

virtue, fulfilment, grace

BIOGRAPHY

A member of a prominent family, Thomas Aquinas (ca. 1225–1274) was expected to pursue a clerical career with the Benedictines and to eventually become the abbot of a major abbey. But in 1244, he decided to join the recently established Order of the Preachers also known as the Dominicans. His family was so dismayed that he was kidnapped and imprisoned in the family castle, although his mother eventually helped him escape. Later in life, Thomas wrote a book entitled

Hasselaar, Jan Jorrit, Mark van Vuuren, Julieta Matos Castaño, and Erik Borgman, eds. *Voices of Hope: Rediscovering and Building Hope for All.* Amsterdam: Amsterdam University Press / Central European University Press, 2026.
 DOI 10.5117/9789048577347-2

Contra impugnantes Dei cultum et religionem [Against Those Who Assail the Worship of God and Religion], in which he defended the Dominican and Franciscan mendicant orders against William of Saint-Amour (ca. 1200–1272), who had attacked their life in poverty and their study of pagan philosophers alongside the Sacred Scripture and the ancient Christian writers.

The Dominicans sent Thomas to study at the Faculty of the Arts at the University of Paris. There he met Albert the Great (Albertus Magnus, ca. 1200–1280), who became his main teacher. When Albert was sent to Cologne, Thomas followed him there. Tradition has it that because Thomas was quiet and did not speak much, he was considered slow. However, Albert supposedly exclaimed prophetically: 'You call him the dumb ox, but in his teaching he will one day produce such a bellowing that it will be heard throughout the world.'

Between 1257 and 1259, Thomas was regent of the Dominican students in Paris. He returned for a second term from 1269 to 1272. His second tenure was marked by major conflicts between the so-called Averroists, who adhered to an Aristotelian philosophy separated from the Christian faith, and the so-called Augustinians, who wanted to ban the philosophy of Aristotle altogether. Aquinas defended the possibility of an orthodox doctrine based on Aristotle, who he generally refers to in his writings as 'the Philosopher'. After leaving for Naples, Thomas had a vision in 1273, after which he likened everything he had ever written to 'straw'. From that point on, although he had been a prolific writer, he stopped writing altogether. Thomas Aquinas died on his way to the Council of Lyon.

In 1277, some of Thomas's theses were condemned, but this condemnation was revoked when Pope John XXII canonized him in 1323. Pope Pius V, himself a Dominican, declared Aquinas a Doctor of the Church in 1567. In 1879, Pope Leo XIII, through his encyclical *Aeterni Patris*, declared Aquinas's oeuvre the normative exposition of Catholic doctrine. Neo-Thomism became a major weapon against anti-Christian modern philosophy and 'modernist' theology.

THOMAS AQUINAS ON HOPE

Aquinas wrote about hope on different occasions. Here, I will present his doctrine as developed in his magnum opus, the *Summa Theologiae.* Although his way of reasoning is rather abstract, what he wrote has profound implications. The key insight is this: a life in faith is a life of hope for eternal community with God, which brings human beings eternal happiness.

According to Aquinas, hope is a virtue. For him, this means the right ordering of the natural human passions. It is natural for human beings to strive for something they want but do not yet have. In Aquinas's view, hope differs from simple desire in that it is directed towards a future good – and not just something seemingly attractive – that is difficult but not impossible to obtain (I-II, Q. 40, Art. 1). Aquinas believed that human beings were created for perfect (that is: eternal) happiness. Anything less will ultimately always leave us unsatisfied. Now, eternal happiness is not something human beings can realize by themselves. Hope is virtuous, according to Aquinas, in that it directs us to God, both for assistance to obtain this ultimate end and as the proper end itself (II-II, Q. 17, Art. 1). Since the essence of God's goodness is imparting good things to his creatures, hoping for eternal happiness in fact means hoping for God, who alone can give it to us (Art. 2). Having God as its object turns hope into a 'theological virtue' (Art. 5). Aquinas distinguishes between ends proportionate to human nature that can be obtained by means of our human capacities and ends that surpass human nature. The latter can only be obtained by the power of God, that is, by participation in the divine nature, promised to us in Christ (I-II, Q. 62, Art. 1; cf. 2 Peter 1: 4).

The fact that, for Aquinas, hope has eternal happiness as its final end and relies on divine assistance as its ultimate cause does not preclude us from placing our hope in other human beings. God is the first cause, but human beings can be secondary causes by helping us to obtain God's help, for instance by praying for us or by encouraging us to go on hoping (II-II, Q. 17, Art. 4). Aquinas also believes that we can hope for one another. If we love another person, we can desire something for him or her with the same intensity as we desire it for ourselves. Thus, we can hope for eternal happiness for another person (Art. 8). This leads him to a remarkable conclusion. He writes: '[J]ust as it is the same virtue of charity whereby a person loves God, himself, and his neighbour, so too it is the same virtue of hope whereby one hopes for himself and for another.' (Art. 3). Although not stated in so many words, this suggests that ultimately, hope is the hope for eternal happiness for all human beings. This accords with God's ultimate intention: 'God ... wants everyone to be saved' (1 Timothy 2: 3–4).

Because hope is equivalent to desiring God's help to reach eternal happiness through communion with God, hope presupposes faith, according to Thomas (Art. 7). Hope leads to love in the sense that it teaches us to love the One that is able and willing to give us the highest good. However, hope also presupposes love because to expect this gift from God implies that we consider God our friend, and being friends presupposes mutual love (Art. 8).

That hope is a virtue implies that it resides in the will. Hope means having a steadfast will to gain eternal happiness (Q. 15, Art. 1). At the same time, hope is based on insight: the insight that God is our helper and that, by consequence, eternal happiness is possible with God's help. We gain these insights through faith, which resides above all in the cognitive faculty. For Aquinas (Art. 2), hope derives its certainty from the fact that faith in God is our response to God revealing Himself in Jesus Christ as love (cf. 1 John 4:4). Further, in his Commentary on Saint Paul's Letter to the Romans, Aquinas clarifies how it is through the Holy Spirit that we are made participants in God's love. In Aquinas's understanding, the Holy Spirit is the mutual love between the Father and the Son (he is following Augustine here). By this participation through the Holy Spirit, we ourselves become lovers of God. When Divine Wisdom says, 'I love those who love me' (Prov. 8:17), Aquinas interprets this to mean that our love of God is a sign that God loves us.

Because hope for eternal happiness is an expression of us loving God through our participation in his love for us, Aquinas (echoing Saint Paul) states that our hope will not be disappointed (Super ad Romanos, Caput 5, Lectio 1; Romans 5:5). We already have what we hope for – or rather, God in whom we hope already has us – in our hope. This does not mean that it is impossible for us to lose hope and thus to fail to attain the happiness for which we were created. It does mean that if we remain in hope, our hope will not be in vain.

REFERENCES AND BIBLIOGRAPHICAL INFORMATION

Kerr, F. (2009). *Thomas Aquinas: A Very Short Introduction*. Oxford, England: Oxford University Press.

Turner, D. (2013). *Thomas Aquinas: A Portrait*. New Haven, CT: Yale University Press.

Thomas Aquinas. (n.d.). *Works of Thomas Aquinas* (Latin and English translations). https://isidore.co/aquinas/

ABOUT THE AUTHOR

Erik Borgman is a lay Dominican and professor emeritus of public theology at Tilburg University, the Netherlands.

FREDERICK DOUGLASS

Hope in finding one's voice and the freedom of becoming

BY JULIETA MATOS CASTAÑO

ARTWORK BY JANWILLEM HOFTIJZER

ABSTRACT

This essay reflects on how Frederick Douglass discovered hope through reclaiming his voice during oppression. Literacy and moral courage allowed him to transform suffering into strength. His life illustrates hope as an active process of becoming, grounded in truth-telling and the pursuit of freedom.

KEYWORDS

voice, freedom, becoming

BIOGRAPHY

In revisiting the life of Frederick Douglass (1818–1895), we come to know a writer, speaker, and abolitionist whose search for freedom became both his life's work and his way of being in the world. He was born into slavery as Frederick Bailey in Maryland, the son of an enslaved mother and an unknown white man. Denied freedom, he

---

Hasselaar, Jan Jorrit, Mark van Vuuren, Julieta Matos Castaño, and Erik Borgman, eds. *Voices of Hope: Rediscovering and Building Hope for All.* Amsterdam: Amsterdam University Press / Central European University Press, 2026.
 DOI 10.5117/9789048577347-3

was also stripped of the right to shape his own life. He was not even allowed to know his date of birth.

Douglass rebelled against his bondage by secretly teaching himself to read and write. His determination to learn opened an inner door, inspiring him to view knowledge as a lifelong act of resistance. Words became his way of making sense of the world and of envisioning possibilities beyond his daily reality.

At age twenty, Frederick broke free and chose to carry his past with him rather than leave it behind. Although this meant reopening wounds, he made a conscious choice to transform his pain into testimony. In his words, he carried his painful experiences and a vision of a better future, painting a horizon full of hope and possibility. Douglass believed that imagination is the soil in which freedom could take root and grow. As his influence grew, he became an essential figure in the abolitionist movement through his speeches, his autobiography *Narrative of the Life of Frederick Douglass, an American Slave* (1845), and his role as editor of the anti-slavery newspaper *The North Star*.

Behind the public figure who moved crowds, there was an introspective man. Through writing, Douglass returned to his memories and did not look away from their brutality. He did the slow, painful work of healing. An essential part of that process was refusing to let hatred shape him and embracing forgiveness as a transformative force in a system designed to hate and tear apart.

His legacy lies in how he managed to continue growing and inspiring others. Having escaped slavery, he still experienced betrayal. Even allies could turn against him, and his political ideas met with fierce resistance. He kept returning to the question: what does it mean to be free and to live with imagination and in connection with others? As a result, he began to understand freedom as a political ideal and an interior practice: if you want to be free, you need to practice becoming true to yourself and others.

FREDERICK DOUGLASS ON HOPE

Douglass's autobiography, *Narrative of the Life of Frederick Douglass, an American Slave*, was published in 1845. In it, he recalls the horrors of slavery, documenting the violence he endured. However, that is not his main purpose. Reading the book feels like entering a meditation on how to hold onto hope in a world where cruelty has been made law. Through language, he reclaims his story and thus restores his humanity, writing how he found his way through life. His firsthand experiences reveal that hope is forged through struggle, requiring a daily choice to embrace it to defy despair.

Early in his life, Douglass recognized that the path to freedom began within himself. In the face of constant attempts at erasure, he held onto this sense of self as a form of hope, making it a patient, intentional practice. This was not a comforting hope to soften pain but rather one that sharpened his awareness and strengthened his endurance, allowing him to keep going.

Mr. Covey was the man tasked with keeping Douglass captive and crushing his spirit. Even at his lowest point, something in Douglass refused to disappear. After a brutal, terrible beating, he decided to fight back physically and spiritually, reclaiming a part of himself that had been buried.

> This battle with Mr. Covey was the turning-point in my life as a slave. It rekindled the few expiring embers of freedom and revived within me a sense of my own manhood. It recalled the departed self-confidence and inspired me again with a determination to be free. (Douglass, 1845, ch. 10)

In that moment of resistance, Douglass's hope emerged from his pain and from his refusal to remain on his knees. But that act of rebellion had already begun years earlier with his determination to learn how to read and write. Literacy opened a door that could never be closed again, and every word he read deepened his understanding of himself and of the system that held him captive.

Literacy did not free him immediately, however. On the contrary. 'I would at times feel that learning to read had been a curse rather than a blessing. It opened my eyes to the horrible pit, but to no ladder upon which to get out.' (Douglass, 1845, ch.7). It nonetheless changed how he perceived, acted, and moved through the world, allowing him to gain a sense that something else was possible. Teaching others to read in secret was one way he resisted Covey's attempts to break him. Resistance became a daily practice. One of his most famous lines, from a speech in 1857, is often quoted as a rallying cry: 'If there is no struggle, there is no progress.'

Imagining freedom while the world denies it is already an act of resistance. And in that act, hope gains ground. Douglass's work reveals that within the same interior space that nurtured hope, forgiveness is also a powerful force. Forgiveness was a conscious refusal to let hatred rule him, acting as a form of freedom emerging from within that kept his integrity intact. He forgave others as a commitment to the humanity that injustice tried to erase in vain. A telling example is how Douglass reflected on how the brutalizing and denigrating force of slavery deformed not only the enslaved but also the enslavers. Reflecting on the woman who had once tried to teach him to read, he writes:

> Slavery soon proved its ability to divest her of these heavenly qualities. Under its influence, the tender heart became stone, and the lamblike disposition gave way to one of tiger-like fierceness (Douglass, 1845, ch. 17).

Instead of retreating in anger or rage, he made the decision to confront the harsh reality: slavery caused harm to both enslavers and the enslaved. Accepting this required extraordinary moral strength, but in doing so, Douglass showed that hope and forgiveness are not about softening reality or denying its damage but about staying present in the struggle.

Today, when we look at portraits of Douglass, his eyes show the strength of someone who has witnessed horror and carried an unbroken will, reminding us that hope, when chosen, is actually a form of freedom in itself. For Douglass, this freedom went beyond laws or emancipation papers and embraced a spiritual and emotional regeneration to reclaim the right to imagine. Achieving freedom, therefore, involved a lengthy and deliberate process of repairing the wounds left by enslavement, both internally and externally. At the end of his autobiography, Douglass reaches the North. Instead of treating it as an arrival, he makes it the start of his commitment to the constant work of freedom.

REFERENCES AND BIBLIOGRAPHICAL INFORMATION

Blight, D.W. (2020). *Frederick Douglass: Prophet of Freedom.* Simon & Schuster.

Douglass, F. (1845). *Narrative of the Life of Frederick Douglass, an American slave.*

(Original work published 1845)

Douglass, F. (1852). *What to the Slave is the Fourth of July?*

Douglass, F. (1853). *The Heroic Slave.*

Douglass, F. (1855). *My Bondage and My Freedom.*

Douglass, F. (1857). West India emancipation speech.

Douglass, F. (1893). *Life and Times of Frederick Douglass.* (Revised edition; original work published 1881)

Library of America. (2023). *The Frederick Douglass Collection* (Vols. 1–2).

ABOUT THE AUTHOR

Julieta Matos Castaño is a research associate at Vrije Universiteit Amsterdam and a practitioner in the field of futures thinking and design at Futures Compass, based in the Netherlands.

REINHOLD NIEBUHR

Saved by hope

BY ANDRIES BOUWMAN AND TRINEKE PALM

ARTWORK BY JANWILLEM HOFTIJZER

ABSTRACT

This essay explains Reinhold Niebuhr's view of hope rooted in grace. According to Niebuhr, hope encourages us to embrace imperfection and to engage responsibly with a fractured world. Hope gives us consciousness and virtue, helping us to make wise and graceful choices in the face of uncertainty.

KEYWORDS

imperfection, responsibility, grace

INTRODUCTION

Reinhold Niebuhr (1892–1971) was a German-American theologian, philosopher, and political scientist. He spent most of his life as a professor of ethics at Union Theological Seminary, where he taught Dietrich Bonhoeffer, among others, during the latter's studies in the United States (1930–1931). Niebuhr is best described as a preacher–activist. His life was marked by his theologically inspired criticism of social – and especially political – developments around him.

Hasselaar, Jan Jorrit, Mark van Vuuren, Julieta Matos Castaño, and Erik Borgman, eds. *Voices of Hope: Rediscovering and Building Hope for All.* Amsterdam: Amsterdam University Press / Central European University Press, 2026.

 DOI 10.5117/9789048577347-4

He did not shy away from joining political movements, nor from openly criticizing them. As a result, he frequently changed his stance. He flirted with liberalism, pacifism, and Marxism. While he acknowledged valuable elements in these ideologies, he also criticized their fundamental assumptions: the self-centredness of liberalism and the complete subordination of the individual in Marxism. He did not hesitate to voice these critiques from the pulpit. For example, he supported Martin Luther King's critique of the Vietnam War.

Thanks to his lively preaching style, he quickly gained recognition in various religious circles. He built a large and influential network of political leaders, industrialists, and labour union leaders. His appeal to these powerful individuals lay in the way he held up a mirror to them in their search for ways to act morally and to take responsibility in an immoral society. He explored this theme in his book *Moral Man and Immoral Society* (1932).

His brother Richard, also a theologian, pushed him to further develop his anthropology. In his magnum opus, *The Nature and Destiny of Man* (1943), Reinhold Niebuhr argued that as children of nature, humans are sinful, subject to unpredictable whims, and driven by needs and impulses. Yet we are also spiritual beings, created in the image of God, and thus capable of reason and of hope to improve the world we live in.

From his theological view on human nature and destiny, Niebuhr developed a Christian approach to social issues and international politics, known as Christian realism. In his book *The Children of Light and the Children of Darkness* (1944), he tried to find a middle way between cynicism and idealism. He raised awareness of our ruthless self-interest but also pointed out our capacity to pursue the theological ideals of faith, hope, and love. He warned against calls for absolute, perfect justice. At the same time, he did not shrink from addressing issues of structural injustice in his own age. He called for relative justice: finding the right balance between what must be done and what is possible. We may not be able to realize paradise on earth, but we should do what is in our power to slow down the desecration of God's creation. So, despite and amidst all our human constraints, Niebuhr emphasized our responsibility to make a difference in situations of health and sickness, war and peace.

The Irony of American History (1952) is Niebuhr's last major work and is considered his most influential. When he wrote it, the United States felt supremely powerful and claimed moral leadership. Niebuhr held up a mirror to the nation, arguing that this self-satisfied attitude leads to ironic blind spots regarding its own moral weaknesses.

Already in his lifetime, Niebuhr was widely recognized for the impact of his writings. He was on the cover of *Time Magazine* in 1948. And in 1991 he was again celebrated as 'the greatest Protestant theologian in America since Jonathan Edwards'. His writings have influenced political leaders ranging from Presidents Jimmy Carter and Barack Obama to Senator John McCain.

Apart from his impact on political leaders, intellectuals, and theologians, Reinhold Niebuhr's legacy lives on in the lives of many ordinary people through the Serenity Prayer that he composed: 'O God, give us the serenity to accept what cannot be changed, the courage to change what can be changed, and the wisdom to know the one from the other.'

REINHOLD NIEBUHR ON HOPE

> Nothing that is worth doing can be achieved in our lifetime; therefore we must be saved by hope. Nothing which is true or beautiful or good makes complete sense in any immediate context of history; therefore we must be saved by faith. Nothing we do, however virtuous, can be accomplished alone; therefore we are saved by love. No virtuous act is quite as virtuous from the standpoint of our friend or foe as it is from our standpoint. Therefore we must be saved by the final form of love which is forgiveness. (Niebuhr, 1952)

Hopeful is not the first adjective that comes to mind when reading Niebuhr's work, with its emphasis on human sinfulness, lust for power, and broken structures. Yet, as this quote underscores, hope is a critical – though subtle – ingredient in the recipe of Niebuhr's political philosophy.

Crucially, his understanding of hope is rooted in grace. The hope of resurrection and the receptiveness to grace enable us to embrace our destiny as children of God and to trust in God and in one another. It keeps us away from both fanatic idealism (a Messiah complex) and pessimistic resignation. Hope as grace enables us to deal with the impermanence and imperfection of the world we live in, to persevere in doing good because we are able to envisage a better world beyond our lifetime.

Robin Lovin, a retired ethics professor, identifies three ways in which hope features in Niebuhr's writings. Hope gives us the *consciousness* that things can change. It anticipates change even beyond our lifetime. Hope is a *law* that sets a norm for acting and taking responsibility for other people, even when we do not feel any connection to these other people. And hope is a *virtue* that, through grace, turns into a habit for making wise choices in times of great uncertainty.

As Niebuhr already demonstrated himself during his lifetime, this understanding of hope is not just theory – it also has political implications. For example, Niebuhr's account of hope beyond history is meaningful in the context of ecological politics. Rather than 'sponsoring environmental indolence and disregard, [it] underscores the promise, prudence, and duty of diligently pursuing ecological protection and rehabilitation' (Simmons 2023, p. 46). With Niebuhr in mind, we may conclude that 'hope is not the negation of pessimism, but its sublation' (Ibid. 47).

REFERENCES AND BIBLIOGRAPHICAL INFORMATION

Lovin, R.W. (2022). 'Hope, Virtue, and Politics in Reinhold Niebuhr's Works.' In K. Carnahan & D. True (Eds.), *Paradoxical Virtues: Reinhold Niebuhr and the Virtues* (33–47). Lanham, MD: Lexington Books.

Niebuhr, R. (1932). *Moral Man and Immoral Society: A Study in Ethics and Politics*. New York: Charles Scribner's Sons.

Niebuhr, R. (1941–1943). *The Nature and Destiny of Man: A Christian Interpretation* (Vols. 1–2). New York: Charles Scribner's Sons.

Niebuhr, R. (1944). *The Children of Light and the Children of Darkness: A Vindication of Democracy and a Critique of its Traditional Defense*. New York: Charles Scribner's Sons.

Niebuhr, R. (1952). *The Irony of American History*. New York: Charles Scribner's Sons.

Sabella, J.L. (2017). *An American Conscience: The Reinhold Niebuhr Story*. Grand Rapids, MI: Eerdmans.

Simmons, F.V. (2023). 'Environmental Ethics and Christian Realism.' In D. Gingles, K. Carnahan, & R.H. Tuttle (Eds.), *The Future of Christian Realism: Adaptations and Continuities* (136–160). Lanham, MD: Lexington Books.

ABOUT THE AUTHORS

Andries Bouwman is mayor of Opsterland, a rural municipality in the north of the Netherlands.

Trineke Palm is director of the think tank of the ChristenUnie, a Dutch Christian-social political party.

VIKTOR FRANKL

Hoping as a response to the circumstances of life

BY MARK VAN VUUREN

ARTWORK BY JANWILLEM HOFTIJZER

ABSTRACT

This essay explores Viktor Frankl's view of hope as something that arises through meaning. Hope is a verb; it is an act of hoping. Even in severe hardship, humans can choose their stance toward the conditions of life and respond to the questions of meaning that our lives are asking of us.

KEYWORDS

meaning, choice, response

BIOGRAPHY

Viktor Frankl (1905–1997) was an Austrian neurologist, psychiatrist, and Holocaust survivor. Born in Vienna in 1905, Frankl showed an early interest in psychology. Corresponding with Sigmund Freud as a teenager and later aligning more closely with Alfred Adler's school of thought, he ultimately developed his own approach.

Hasselaar, Jan Jorrit, Mark van Vuuren, Julieta Matos Castaño, and Erik Borgman, eds. *Voices of Hope: Rediscovering and Building Hope for All.* Amsterdam: Amsterdam University Press / Central European University Press, 2026.
 DOI 10.5117/9789048577347-5

During World War II, Frankl was interned in four Nazi concentration camps, including Auschwitz. He lost his wife, parents, and brother in the Holocaust. These experiences deeply influenced his understanding of human resilience and the will to find meaning even in the most harrowing circumstances. When he arrived in Auschwitz, he was carrying with him his manuscript introducing what would later become known as logotherapy. This manuscript was taken from him and immediately destroyed. Despite this, he clung to hope: the hope that his wife would survive the women's camp (she did not) and that he would survive to publish his destroyed manuscript (which he did, calling the book *The Doctor and the Soul*).

It was in this book that Frankl wrote about the freedom to choose for hope: 'Everything can be taken from a man but one thing: the last of the human freedoms – to choose one's attitude in any given set of circumstances, to choose one's own way.' As absurd as it may seem, Frankl observed Auschwitz even as he endured it as a prisoner. He took a 'professional interest' in how people survived. It was clear how people died there. The whole system was designed to dehumanize prisoners, kill them, and eradicate entire groups. But can one survive in such a situation? Frankl found two elements crucial for survival: pure luck and deep hope.

After the war, Viktor Frankl resumed his career in Vienna and became a professor of neurology and psychiatry. He is the founder of logotherapy, a form of existential analysis that emphasizes the human search for meaning as the central motivational force in life. This school of psychotherapy focuses on logos (i.e. meaning), asking for clarity about people's search for a meaningful future. This meaning is not readily available to everyone but rather something that one must find: what question are you striving to be the answer to? Meaning is fulfilled in the future a person actively strives to bring about. He chronicled his insights in his seminal book published in 1946, *Man's Search for Meaning*, which became one of the most influential psychological texts of the twentieth century.

Viktor Frankl died at the age of 92, leaving behind a powerful legacy of hope, dignity, and the enduring human capacity to find purpose, even in suffering.

VIKTOR FRANKL ON HOPE

According to Frankl, the major source of hope lies in identifying one's will to meaning. Citing Nietzsche, he wrote that someone 'who has a Why to live for, can bear almost any How'. This does not mean that life becomes easy – on the contrary. Meaning means facing tensions:

> I consider it a dangerous misconception of mental hygiene to assume that what man needs in the first place is equilibrium [...] a tensionless state. What man actually needs is not a tensionless state but rather the striving and struggling for a worthwhile goal, a freely chosen task. What he needs is not the discharge of tension at any cost but the call of a potential meaning waiting to be fulfilled by him.

In other words, hope hurts because 'what wants to give light, must endure burning'. But burning is to be preferred over meaninglessness. Without a Why, almost any How (the circumstances of one's life) will be felt as miserable.

Hope needs to be expressed in oneself, especially when no hope can be drawn from external circumstances: 'When we are no longer able to change a situation, we are challenged to change ourselves.' Illusionary hope for a change in one's circumstance could even be lethal. Frankl describes how a fellow inmate in the camp shared a dream he had in February 1945 that they would be liberated on 30 March. This dreamer's hope was strong until it became highly unlikely that the end of March would bring freedom. He fell ill on 30 March and died the day after. Frankl concludes that:

> the ultimate cause of my friend's death was that the expected liberation did not come and he was severely disappointed. This suddenly lowered his body's resistance against the latent typhus infection. His faith in

> the future and his will to live had become paralyzed and his body fell victim to illness.

In this case, losing hope had turned into a death sentence.

During his stay in Auschwitz, Victor Frankl had a few opportunities to explain his logotherapy to his friends in the barracks. Such an opportunity arose in the midst of random punishments for minor offenses. This example, reported in *Man's Search for Meaning*, is a good summary of Frankl's sources of meaning and hope. He writes how the senior block warden

> talked about the many comrades who had died in the last few days, either of sickness or of suicide. But he also mentioned what may have been the real reason for their deaths: giving up hope. He maintained that there should be some way of preventing possible future victims from reaching this extreme state and it was to me that the warden pointed to give this advice.

Next, Frankl summarizes his speech in four sections. First, he mentions

> the most trivial of comforts, [...] namely that our situation was not the most terrible we could think of. I said that each of us had to ask himself what irreplaceable losses he had suffered up to then. I speculated that for most of them these losses had really been few. Whoever was still alive had reason for hope. [...] After all, we still had all our bones intact. Whatever we had gone through could still be an asset for us in the future.

Secondly, Frankl spoke about how the future must seem hopeless.

> I agreed that each of us could guess for himself how small were his chances of survival. I told him that I estimated my own chances at about one in twenty, but I also told him that in spite of this I had no intention of losing hope and giving up. For no man knew what the future would bring much less the next hour.

Next, after talking about the future and the veil that was drawn over it, Frankl translates the past into hope. He talks about the past:

> all its joys and how its light shone even in the present darkness. [...] All we have done, whatever great thoughts we may have had, and all we have suffered, All this is not lost, though it is past; we have brought it into being. Having been is also a kind of being, and perhaps the surest kind.

Frankl then spoke of the many opportunities of giving life a meaning.

> I told my comrades that human life under any circumstances never ceases to have a meaning and that this infinite meaning of life includes suffering and dying, privation and death. [...] [Facing] up to the seriousness of our position, they must not lose hope but should keep their courage in the certainty that the hopelessness of our struggle did not detract from its dignity and its meaning. I said that someone looks down on each of us in different or cold hours – a friend, a wife, somebody alive or dead, or a God – and he would not expect us to disappoint them. He would hope to find us suffering proudly, not miserably, knowing how to die.

He ended by speaking about sacrifice, which in his view had meaning in every case:

> I told him of a comrade who on his arrival in camp had tried to make a pact with Heaven that his suffering and death should save the human being he loved from a painful end. For this man, suffering and death were meaningful. His was a sacrifice of the deepest significance. He did not want to die for nothing. None of us wanted that.

For Viktor Frankl, hope is a verb: hope means hoping. This hoping is not a detached pondering of a question that needs a once-and-for-all conclusive answer. It is not an answer but rather an answering by us: 'We need to stop thinking about the meaning of life,' Frankl writes, 'and instead think of ourselves as those who were being questioned by life, daily and hourly.' Hoping thus becomes a continuous process of answering the questions that life continually poses.

REFERENCES AND BIBLIOGRAPHICAL INFORMATION

Frankl, V.E. (1986). *The Doctor and the Soul: From Psychotherapy to Logotherapy*. Vintage. (Original work published 1955)

Frankl, V.E. (2006). *Man's Search for Meaning*. Simon & Schuster. (Original work published 1946)

Frankl, V.E. (2014). *The Will to Meaning: Foundations and Applications of Logotherapy*. Penguin.

Frankl, V.E. (2024). *Embracing Hope: On Freedom, Responsibility, and the Meaning of Life*. Beacon Press.

Längle, A., & Sykes, B.M. (2006). 'Viktor Frankl—Advocate for humanity: On his 100th birthday.' *Journal of Humanistic Psychology*, 46(1): 36–47. https://doi.org/10.1177/0022167805281150

ABOUT THE AUTHOR

Mark van Vuuren is associate professor of positive organizing at the University of Twente, the Netherlands.

PAUL RICOEUR

Hopeful language?

BY HENCO VAN DER WESTHUIZEN

ARTWORK BY JANWILLEM HOFTIJZER

ABSTRACT

This essay explores Paul Ricoeur's view of hope as holding together finitude and possibility. Our reality is never fully closed, as we know through metaphors and texts that can continually redescribe the world. Even in darkness, humans retain the capacity to imagine otherwise and begin again, becoming an affirmation that meaning and renewal remain possible.

KEYWORDS

imagination, possibility, renewal

'*... language could extend itself to its very limits, forever discovering new resonances within itself*'

BIOGRAPHY

Paul Ricoeur (1913–2005) was a French philosopher whose long life and work centred around questions of philosophical anthropology. His thinking navigates between a clear-sighted diagnosis of our limits, fallibility, and vulnerability and a quiet confidence in the possibil-

Hasselaar, Jan Jorrit, Mark van Vuuren, Julieta Matos Castaño, and Erik Borgman, eds. *Voices of Hope: Rediscovering and Building Hope for All.* Amsterdam: Amsterdam University Press / Central European University Press, 2026.

 DOI 10.5117/9789048577347-6

ity of meaning and understanding. In fact, this is where hope enters his philosophy.

Ricoeur was raised in a strict Protestant household in Rennes that instilled Bible reading, study, and discipline. From a very early age, his world became the world of words and texts. After studying in Rennes and Paris, he passed the demanding *agrégation* examination and became a philosophy teacher.

The Second World War marked him deeply. Called up as an officer, he was captured in 1940 and spent almost five years in prisoner-of-war camps. There he read philosophy intensively, translated Husserl's *Ideas I* (in tiny handwriting in order to save paper), and drafted his first major work, *Freedom and Nature*. Surviving while others died made him determined never to take his life for granted. Intellectually, the camp years planted in him a lifelong quest to comprehend evil, finitude, and the possibility of meaning.

PAUL RICOEUR ON HOPE

Ricoeur seeks to describe the basic abilities that make responsible action and shared life possible – speaking, acting, narrating, and imagining – while never denying our vulnerability. We are never fully transparent to ourselves; we know ourselves only through our relations to the world, to others, and to history.

His early work shows how a basic disproportion runs through us: our aspirations reach beyond what we can actually do. This does not lead him to apathy but instead raises the question of how we can still act. To answer it, he turns to language, symbols, and texts. In *The Symbolism of Evil*, for example, he argues that evil is always spoken of indirectly – through images. Hence his famous claim that the symbol gives rise to thought. In order to understand ourselves, we must interpret the signs and the stories that have been handed down to us by tradition.

From here, his work opens up into a broad hermeneutics. He stresses the fullness of language and its many meanings. Real language is never completely clear or one-dimensional; it always calls for interpretation. Ricoeur develops a conversation between a hermeneutics that trusts the meanings carried by symbols and a critical hermeneutics that unmasks hidden distortions and ideologies. Instead of choosing between them, he treats critique and trust as necessary partners.

In the 1970s and 1980s, narrative became central. Ricoeur's book *Time and Narrative* explores how stories weave events into meaningful wholes and how this helps us understand both history and our own lives. Later, in *Oneself as Another*, he claims that we become who we are through the stories we tell and those told about us, always in relation to others. His last works on memory, history, forgetting, and recognition ask whether mutual recognition is still possible in the face of trauma.

Hope in Ricoeur is *rarely* thematized as a standalone concept. Rather, it operates implicitly through his hermeneutics itself. Throughout his work, hope appears in the way Ricoeur holds together finitude and possibility. Our actions and words are shaped by given contexts, yet they can also reach beyond the way things now stand, giving voice to new meanings and as yet unrealized possibilities. His lifelong commitment to interpretation assumes that language, symbols, and narratives can continue to disclose fresh sense; our self-understanding and our shared world are not closed.

This brings us to one key text where his hermeneutical vision and his quiet hope meet most clearly: the study on 'Métaphore et référence' in *La Métaphore Vive* [The Rule of Metaphor]. Here he shows how metaphor allows language to reimagine the world – and why that matters for rediscovering hope.

In *The Rule of Metaphor* (the translation of the book title misses the *vive*, which means alive, living, vivid, vital), he asks: when we use metaphors, do we only play with words, or do we really say something about the world? His answer will show why he thinks hope can be grounded in language itself.

Ricoeur starts by making a distinction. He says we must distinguish between a sign (*signe*) and discourse (*discours*). A sign is a word taken inside a language system, like a dictionary entry. A word on its own only points to other words; its life is inside the language. Discourse is different. Discourse is language in use: sentences spoken or written by someone, at some time, about something. Discourse is *about* things. This distinction is crucial. If we stay only with signs, we can never move beyond language. But if we pay attention to discourse, we can see how language reaches out toward the world. This is important for hope because it means language is not a closed circle; it is directed toward reality.

Next, Ricoeur takes up two further terms: sense (*sens*) and reference (*référence*). Sense is what a sentence means inside the language; reference is what that sentence is about in the world. 'The bird is on the branch' has a sense (we understand the structure of the sentence) and a reference (there is a bird and a branch arranged in a certain way). We use language not only to juggle meanings inside our heads but because we care about truth, about saying something *about* reality. That concern for truth pushes us from sense to reference.

Now Ricoeur turns to metaphor. A metaphor is a sentence where words are used in an unusual way: 'Hope is a bird.' Taken literally, such sentences are false or even nonsense. Hope has no feathers. In a metaphor, the usual sense of the words breaks down. But Ricoeur notices something important: that breakdown is not the end of meaning; it is the beginning. When we hear 'Hope is a bird', our mind does not stop. It looks for another way to understand the sentence. We start to see hope as something that lifts us, moves lightly ahead of us, and carries a new horizon, like a bird. So, the literal sense is destroyed but a new, richer sense appears.

What happens to reference here? Many philosophers and critics have said: in poetic language there is no reference, only sense. In this view, metaphors may move us but they do not tell us anything about reality. Ricoeur thinks this is wrong. He agrees that metaphors suspend the usual, straightforward references. When we say 'Hope is a bird', we are not pointing to an object in the way we do in the sentence 'The bird is on a branch.' Ordinary, descriptive reference is put in brackets. But that suspension has a purpose. It makes possible a *new* way of pointing to the world. We are now directed not to an object but to a way of seeing hope as something that lifts us and moves us toward the future. In other words, metaphor gives us a different kind of reference: the reference of a possible world.

To make this clearer, Ricoeur shifts from single sentences to whole texts. A text is more than a string of sentences; it is a work with a beginning, middle, and end, with a certain style and genre. A text, he says, projects *a world in front of it*. When we read a poem, a story, or even a parable, we are invited into a world that the text opens. Interpretation is not just decoding words; it is entering that world and letting it question and reshape us. This is where Ricoeur's idea of hope becomes easier to see. If texts can project possible worlds, then our own world is not fixed once and for all. Literature shows us that reality can be redescribed. There are other ways of being-in-the-world than the ones we currently live.

At this point, it helps to distinguish more clearly between poetic metaphors and scientific models. Poetic metaphors open new ways of seeing and inhabiting possible worlds; they redescribe reality by inviting the imagination into alternative horizons of meaning. Scientific models, by contrast, function as heuristic fictions through simplification and idealization, oriented toward explanation, calculation, and prediction. Both are forms of *fiction*, but they do different kinds of work and aim at different kinds of truth.

This is the heart of his argument. *Metaphor does not merely explain the world; it refigures it*. It is an event in language that both breaks and remakes sense; it suspends ordinary reference to open a new kind of reference; it projects a possible world in which we can recognize new aspects of reality and of ourselves. Language, in this view, is not finished. It can *extend itself to its very limits, forever discovering new resonances within itself.* That is why this study matters for an understanding of hope. If metaphors and texts can continually redescribe the world, then our world is never completely closed. Even in difficult, dark, or evil situations, there remains a basic human capacity to say things differently, to imagine otherwise, and thus to begin to live *otherwise.* In Ricoeur's hands, the theory of metaphor becomes an affirmation that meaning and renewal are still possible.

REFERENCES AND BIBLIOGRAPHICAL INFORMATION

Kearney, R. (2004). *On Paul Ricoeur: The Owl of Minerva.* Ashgate Publishing.

Reagan, C.E. (1996). *Paul Ricoeur: His Life and His Work.* University of Chicago Press.

Ricoeur, P. (1967). *The Symbolism of Evil* (Original work published in 1960). Harper and Row.

Ricoeur, P. (1970). *Freud and Philosophy: An Essay on Interpretation* (Original work published in 1965). Yale University Press.

Ricoeur, P. (1978). *The Rule of Metaphor: Multi-Disciplinary Studies of the Creation of Meaning in Language* (Original work published in 1975). Routledge and Kegan Paul.

Ricoeur, P. (1984–1988). *Time and Narrative* (K. McLaughlin & D. Pellauer, Trans.; Vols. 1–3) (Original work published in 1983–1985). University of Chicago Press.

Ricoeur, P. (1992). *Oneself as Another* (Original work published in 1990). University of Chicago Press.

Ricoeur, P. (2004). *Memory, History, Forgetting.* University of Chicago Press.

ABOUT THE AUTHOR

Henco van der Westhuizen is associate professor in systematic theology at the University of the Free State, South Africa and consultant for the Faith and Order Commission (World Council of Churches).

ETTY HILLESUM

Hope as inner resistance

BY JULIETA MATOS CASTAÑO

ARTWORK BY JANWILLEM HOFTIJZER

ABSTRACT

This essay reflects on Etty Hillesum's cultivation of hope during Nazi persecution. Through introspection and an openness to beauty around her even under the hardest conditions, she created meaning amid terror. Her diaries portray hope as inner resistance, sustained by a sense of presence and responsibility toward others.

KEYWORDS

resistance, presence, compassion

BIOGRAPHY

Esther (Etty) Hillesum (1914–1943) was a Jewish Dutch writer. Her published diaries and letters, written between 1941 and 1943, offer an intimate portrait of hope in the midst of widespread destruction and despair.

She was born in Middelburg and moved to Amsterdam to study law, psychology, and Russian. She lived a vibrant and intellectual existence. Exceptionally bright and curious, her diaries reflect a young

---

Hasselaar, Jan Jorrit, Mark van Vuuren, Julieta Matos Castaño, and Erik Borgman, eds. *Voices of Hope: Rediscovering and Building Hope for All.* Amsterdam: Amsterdam University Press / Central European University Press, 2026.
 DOI 10.5117/9789048577347-7

woman deeply engaged with classical philosophy and psychology, and her portraits reveal this inner life through a luminous, introspective gaze, both dreamy and alert. She was murdered in Auschwitz at the age of 29.

In the years before she was killed, she documented life in Amsterdam under Nazi occupation and in the Westerbork transit camp. She wrote about her everyday experiences: walking through the silent streets of Amsterdam during curfew, enduring the overcrowded barracks, and reflecting on the moment she first put on the yellow Star of David. Hillesum documented the horrors of persecution, the tragedy of her fate, and the transformation that shaped her final years.

As her world closed in, she refused to let violence harden her or define her identity. Instead, she decided to devote herself to cultivating an inner space: a spiritual practice that consisted of being radically present to reality and seeking meaning and lessons hidden in each moment. We witness how Hillesum refused to give in to hatred, insisting that she still carried a seemingly small but powerful freedom to choose how she met and endured suffering and tragedy. She wrote:

> They can harass us, they can rob us of our material goods, of our freedom of movement [...]. We may of course be sad and depressed by what has been done to us; that is only human and understandable. However: our greatest injury is one we inflict upon ourselves. I find life beautiful, and I feel free. (Hillesum 1999, p. 177)

Her writings are far from devoid of suffering. Etty Hillesum invites us to face the darkness she lived without softening its edges. In doing so, we encounter humiliation and despair, and we witness how she chooses a persevering, defiant connection to life itself. As she wrote:

> Do not relieve your feelings through hatred [..]. And if you have given sorrow the space its gentle origins demand, then you may truly say: life is beautiful and so rich. (Hillesum 1999, p. 118)

Knowing she could not 'save' the world, Hillesum kept offering what she could: growth, presence, attention, and a breathing space where humanity could survive.

ETTY HILLESUM ON HOPE

In *An Interrupted Life*, hope and devastation live side by side, shaped by nightly raids, deportations, and the fear of the next knock on the door. Hillesum confronts us with the horrors around her in all their rawness. She writes candidly about the endless transport trains. Through them, we encounter the sick children, the terrified families, and the cruelty that shaped their fate. In this environment, she presents hope as a force that can grow when we refuse to escape from suffering and stay rooted in life while it breaks apart.

Hillesum did not consider herself a victim. She understood early on that peace could no longer be found in the streets, so it would have to be reclaimed within herself. As her surroundings grew more oppressive, fenced in by barbed wire, her inner life kept expanding. Each day, she turned toward the world within her in response to the one crumbling around her: 'The sky within me is as wide as the one stretching above my head.' (Hillesum 1999, p. 177).

Hope, for Hillesum, meant seeing the world exactly as it was, with all its cruelty, and still choosing to respond with courage and care, refusing to deny reality or hate those who were causing the suffering. Through willpower, she discovered what she called a deep well inside herself. This was a sanctuary that cruelty could not reach and became her source of strength. It was an untouchable place from which she could remain open even as the world around her closed in and descended into destruction.

The hope Hillesum cultivated was forged in – and for – the hardest moments. When the darkness outside deepened, she carried this hope with her to Westerbork, the transit camp from which she would later be deported to Auschwitz. There, she continued to practice presence through daily reflection or compassionate service.

Intentionally, she sought beauty by looking more closely at life itself, finding small, fragile signs of the world still moving: a flower blooming beside the barracks, a bird crossing the sky, a smile shared between prisoners. Through such moments, she showed us that even in the worst and most devastating circumstances, beauty could still be present.

At Westerbork, Etty Hillesum cared for others in everyday ways, writing letters for those too weak or frightened to do so, and sitting with them as they waited for deportation. 'We should be willing to act as a balm for all wounds.' (Hillesum 1999, p. 262) Through gestures such as a word of reassurance, a steady presence, the willingness to truly listen, she created meaning, turning these small acts of care into islands of humanity right in the middle of absolute darkness.

As deportation to the concentration camp neared, Hillesum continued to sharpen her commitment to life, transforming what could have been resignation into an intentional stance of inner freedom. As she wrote:

> Ultimately, we have just one moral duty: to reclaim large areas of peace in ourselves, more and more peace, and to reflect it towards others. And the more peace there is in us, the more peace there will also be in our troubled world (Hillesum 1999, p. 267).

Meaning, Hillesum reminds us, is not something that history and circumstances can hand down to us. We must shape it through the choices we make each day: by listening when it would be easier to turn away, and by remaining open to beauty even when the world offers little reason to do so. In these deliberate acts of care, she shows us how meaning can be created even as everything around us falls apart. Her legacy is how she lived: with open eyes and a well of peace that even Auschwitz could not drain.

REFERENCES AND BIBLIOGRAPHICAL INFORMATION

Hillesum, E. (1999). *An Interrupted Life: The Diaries and Letters of Etty Hillesum,* 1941–1943 (A.J. Pomerans, Trans.). Persephone Books.

Etty Hillesum Cards. (n.d.). *Home*. https://www.ettyhillesum-cards.com/

ABOUT THE AUTHOR

Julieta Matos Castaño is a research associate at Vrije Universiteit Amsterdam and a practitioner in the field of futures thinking and design at Futures Compass, based in the Netherlands.

NELSON MANDELA

Hope that changed the course of a nation

BY DANIËL ANDREW

ARTWORK BY JANWILLEM HOFTIJZER

ABSTRACT

This essay describes Nelson Mandela's understanding of hope as a disciplined commitment to reconciliation and justice. His years of imprisonment forged patience and courage that later guided South Africa's transition. Mandela's leadership shows how hope can transform national life by grounding political action in shared humanity.

KEYWORDS

reconciliation, courage, justice

BIOGRAPHY

Nelson Mandela (1918–2013), the anti-apartheid revolutionary and South Africa's first Black president, championed justice, reconciliation, and human rights, enduring 27 years in prison before leading a peaceful transition to democracy for all.

Nelson Rolihlahla Mandela, more fondly remembered by his clan's name, Madiba, was born on 18 July 1918 into the Thembu royal

Hasselaar, Jan Jorrit, Mark van Vuuren, Julieta Matos Castaño, and Erik Borgman, eds. *Voices of Hope: Rediscovering and Building Hope for All.* Amsterdam: Amsterdam University Press / Central European University Press, 2026.

 DOI 10.5117/9789048577347-8

family in Mvezo, South Africa. He studied law at the Universities of Fort Hare and Witwatersrand and worked as a lawyer in Johannesburg. In 1943, Mandela joined the African National Congress (ANC) and soon thereafter co-founded the ANC Youth League. When the National Party came to power in 1948 and officially established the Apartheid system, the ANC engaged in a struggle to end this system that privileged the minority whites over against the majority black population. In 1961, Mandela was involved in the founding of the militant uMkhonto we Sizwe, which sought to actively undermine the Apartheid government.

Due to his political involvement, he was arrested several times and released, but after the Rivonia trial in 1962, he was sentenced to life imprisonment. The prison sentence of 27 years was ended by President F.W. De Klerk in 1990, and in 1994 Nelson Mandela became the first democratically elected president of the Republic of South Africa. Mandela and De Klerk were jointly awarded the Nobel Peace Prize (1993) for their commitment to a peaceful transition and establishment of a non-racial, non-sexist, and democratic country. Mandela is recognized internationally for his activism, his eagerness for a negotiated settlement, and his emphasis on reconciliation between the country's racial groups.

In 1986, when Mandela was still in prison, he managed to smuggle out a letter to the South African musician Hugh Masekela, whom he admired greatly. This prompted Masekela to compose the song 'Bring Him Back Home (Nelson Mandela)', which quickly became the unofficial anthem of the anti-Apartheid struggle.

NELSON MANDELA ON HOPE

During the years of struggle against Apartheid and the difficulty of establishing a united nation after so many years of bloodshed, distrust, and division, what was most appreciated about Nelson Mandela was the hope that he represented for a better life for all. Mandela's forgiveness of his former oppressors, his willingness to work with everyone from the far-right to the far-left, and the selfless, servant-leadership style that he embodied in his political party and in government display the values the world needs today. At his funeral, Barack Obama said, 'Mandela makes me want to be a better man.'

We need the same kind of hope inspired by Madiba – a hope grounded in principle, marked by boldness, and tempered by humility. The boldness of Mandela was his ability to stand up against injustice and to fight on behalf of the downtrodden and the marginalized in society. He was willing to do that even if it cost him his life, as he said during the Rivonia trial, in his speech 'I am Prepared to Die', on 20 April 1964:

> During my lifetime I have dedicated myself to this struggle of the African people. I have fought against white domination, and I have fought against black domination. I have cherished the ideal of a democratic and free society in which all persons live together in harmony and with equal opportunities. It is an ideal which I hope to live for and achieve. But if needs be, it is an ideal for which I am prepared to die.

This turned him into a global symbol of resistance to injustice, unfairness, and discrimination.

Mandela's humility was apparent not only in his decision to establish a Government of National Unity (GNU) that included his former oppressors but also in his refusal to accept his full salary, half of which he donated to charity organizations such as the Nelson Mandela Children's Fund. He also declined to run for a second term as president of the country, even though the Constitution of South Africa allowed it and his popularity as 'the father of the nation' meant that he would have easily won the election.

His acts of reconciliation – contested or not – stand as powerful testaments to his commitment to unity. He visited the home of Hendrik Verwoerd's widow in Orania, for example, and he also made a deliberate decision to retain the Springbok emblem on the rugby jersey even though it symbolized years of exclusion and marginalization for Black South Africans in sport. The day he wore the Springbok jersey at the 1995 Rugby World Cup, he united a nation and offered a symbol of hope to a divided world.

Today, South Africa once again has a Government of National Unity, after no political party was able to win an outright majority in the last elections in 2024. The first such GNU was established by Mandela after the ANC won the first democratic elections in 1994. Although some people were disappointed that the ANC had to share power with other parties, Mandela explained in his autobiography, *Long Walk To Freedom*, that this arrangement was in fact the best outcome:

> In fact I was relieved, had we won two-thirds of the vote and been able to write a constitution unfettered by input from others, people would argue we had created an ANC constitution, not a South African constitution. I wanted a true government of national unity.

His willingness to share power and always include the other was his hallmark. This legacy remains visible even now in the kind of political and economic stability the country still enjoys. As Mandela said during his acceptance speech in 1994, 'I am your servant ... it is not the individuals that matter but the collective... This is a time to heal old wounds and build a new South Africa.' And in his autobiography he elaborates that 'I have never lost hope that this great transformation would occur. Not because of the great heroes I have cited but because of the courage of the ordinary men and women of my country.'

A personal note from Daniël, the author of this chapter:

At this juncture in our country and in the rest of the world – when there is so much division and competition for power, for control, for dominance of one group over another and one country over another – let us keep that hope alive. As Mandela wrote in *Long Walk to Freedom*,

> after climbing a great hill, one only finds that there are many more hills to climb. I have taken a moment here to rest, to steal a view of the glorious vista that surrounds me, to look back on the distance I have come. But I can rest only for a moment, for with freedom come responsibilities...

In this chapter, we have also taken some time to rest on a hill with Madiba as a voice of hope and discovered with him the secret. We have looked back over the distance Madiba has travelled, and we take responsibility for the freedom we share with others. Let us not give up hope but continue to hope against hope, no matter how steep the hills are that we must climb locally and globally. Let us sing along with Hugh Masekela, 'Bring back Nelson Mandela/ Bring him back home'. Let his values become part of who we are as leaders and as citizens.

Let those values of selflessness, sacrifice, and commitment to work for the good of others come home; let it become part of our moral leadership that reflects a servant-leadership style and that puts the interest of others above ours. May we be kind and forgiving of one another, and may we fight for justice for those who are marginalized and pushed to the peripheries of society; resisting the dehumanization and 'thingification' of the other and protecting the most vulnerable in our common home, the earth.

In concluding this short reflection, I turn to the words of S. Scott in his tribute to Mandela:

> Madiba, you were our beacon of hope and liberation. Thank you for sharing yourself with us. You have shown us the path, now it is up to us to walk it.

REFERENCES AND BIBLIOGRAPHICAL INFORMATION

Mandela, N.R. (1964, April 20). *I Am Prepared to Die* [Speech].

Mandela, N.R. (1994). *Long Walk to Freedom: The Autobiography of Nelson Mandela*. Abacus.

Nelson Mandela Foundation. (n.d.). *Nelson Mandela Speeches*. https://www.nelsonmandela.org/speeches

Scott, S. (2014). *Mandela: A Tribute*. Western Cape Government.

ABOUT THE AUTHOR

Daniël Andrew is lecturer in the Department of Practical and Missional Theology at the University of the Free State, South Africa.

JÜRGEN MOLTMANN

Suffering hope?

BY HENCO VAN DER WESTHUIZEN

ARTWORK BY JANWILLEM HOFTIJZER

ABSTRACT

This essay examines Jürgen Moltmann's insight that hope does not arise from escaping suffering but from entering it fully. He argues that moments of deepest abandonment can reveal unexpected forms of solidarity and meaning. In this view, hope is born within suffering itself, where despair is met with transformative presence.

KEYWORDS

suffering, solidarity, transformation

BIOGRAPHY

Jürgen Moltmann (1926–2024) became one of the most widely read and frequently discussed Protestant theologians of the last fifty years. Throughout his long academic career, he returned again and again to central themes of Christian faith, interpreting them in ways that addressed the concrete struggles of modern life. Yet he did not let these realities define the whole story. His work consistently pointed to the risen Christ and to the renewing work of God's Spirit in the world

Hasselaar, Jan Jorrit, Mark van Vuuren, Julieta Matos Castaño, and Erik Borgman, eds. *Voices of Hope: Rediscovering and Building Hope for All.* Amsterdam: Amsterdam University Press / Central European University Press, 2026.
 DOI 10.5117/9789048577347-9

as the basis for hope. His influence on contemporary theology has been remarkable. His writings continue to be studied and debated in theology courses in seminaries and universities worldwide.

Moltmann's first major work, *Theologie der Hoffnung* [Theology of Hope], published in 1964, opened a new and exciting chapter in Christian theology. The book was shaped by the events that defined his life and the questions that arose from them. At age sixteen, he was conscripted into military service during the bombing of Hamburg in 1943. As the city burned, he witnessed his closest friend die beside him. These experiences left him with deep questions about the meaning of human life in the face of overwhelming suffering.

In 1945, he was captured by British forces and spent the next three years in prisoner-of-war camps. It was in one of these camps that he received a Bible and encountered the forsaken and crucified Christ upon reading the Gospels. He later said that it was through this story that he found a language for his own questions and what felt like forsakenness. He discovered a hope that did not bypass suffering but met him within it. It was in the camps that he decided to study theology, not as an escape but as a way of facing the world as it is.

After his release from the camp, he studied, served as a pastor, and then taught theology. The pressing questions of post-war Europe shaped his conviction that theology must speak to real life and help people live toward a future opened by God.

JÜRGEN MOLTMANN ON HOPE

Moltmann's first book, *Theology of Hope*, emerged from his experiences of war, captivity, and theological questioning. In this work, Moltmann argued that Christian faith begins with the resurrection and the future promised by God. Hope for him is not optimism but a power that resists resignation and calls people to transform the world in light of God's future. Eschatology, instead of being an appendix at the end of doctrine, becomes the central way Christians think, believe, pray, and act. The future of God breaks open the closed horizons of history and enables people to imagine and work towards a different world.

This emphasis on hope deepens in his next major book, *The Crucified God* (1972). In it, Moltmann asks his question of God in the forsakenness and suffering of Jesus Christ. He argues that God does not stand above suffering but suffers in and with the crucified Christ. The cross is not a symbol of overpowering but the place where God stands in powerlessness with the forsaken and the suffering of history. Hope is credible only when it stands beside the crucified and refuses a theology that is silent or silences the suffering of others.

In his third major book, *The Church in the Power of the Spirit* (1975), Moltmann turns to the communal implications of this hope, asking what kind of community is formed by the God of the resurrection and the cross. Moltmann describes the church not mainly as an institution but as a movement of the Spirit, called to public witness, to justice and peace, and to life-giving fellowship. As a community of hope, the church lives from God's coming future rather than from the logic of the present.

Together, these three books form a connected whole. Although Moltmann developed a broader systematic theology, these early works were essential in shaping this perspective on hope. They arose from suffering and the conviction that God's future opens where hope seems absent. This conviction comes into focus in Moltmann's lecture *The Passion of God and the Suffering of Christ*, in which he goes back to a fundamental experience in his life: the contradiction between terrible, seemingly meaningless suffering and the search for God.

He begins with two ways that people react to suffering. Some ask a theoretical question: 'How can God allow this?' Others cry out from the deep: 'God, where are you?' These are not the same. The first presupposes a distant God who has to be explained. The second is either looking for a God who is close and *compassionate* or else is on the edge of giving up faith altogether. Moltmann is interested in this cry.

To respond, he does not start with an abstract God. He turns to the central story of Christian faith: the suffering and death of Jesus. He wants first to *see* what happens there, then to *judge* by drawing out what this means for how we talk about God, and finally to *act* and suffer in light of it.

He reads the passion stories as telling us something about Jesus's own experience of God. Two scenes shape his reading: the garden of Gethsemane and the cross on Golgotha. In both places, the question of hope becomes a question about *who God is*.

In Gethsemane, the story says that Jesus was deeply troubled, right up to the moment of his death. Jesus does not go toward his death like an invulnerable *god*. He *is* overwhelmed. Moltmann calls this the struggle in Gethsemane and sees it as a struggle *with* God. The Father who had called him Son seems to have turned away from him, yet Jesus still cries to this God. Already at this point, hope means not letting go of God, even when God seems silent.

On Golgotha, the crucified Christ hangs for hours in what Moltmann calls almost a paralysed state. Then, toward the end, he breaks the silence with his cry, 'My God, my God, why have you forsaken me?' For Moltmann, this is the most important sentence in the whole story. It is not an abstract statement about suffering; it is the experience of abandonment put into words. Jesus does not say simply 'God' but 'my God'. If, at this moment, God were simply absent, Moltmann thinks faith in God would become impossible. The passion story would then be the end of any possible belief in God. The whole lecture depends on a different conviction: that *in* this very cry, God is present – not as a distant god who commands, but as the God who suffers with the crucified one.

Moltmann's theology of the cross is his attempt to hear, inside Jesus's cry, the answer of a compassionate God. Drawing on biblical traditions of exile, he recalls a God who goes with the people into suffering rather than remaining safely above it. Where Christ goes, God goes. What Christ suffers, God suffers. Christ's suffering is caused by human abandonment and violence, yet it is also the place where God freely takes the side of the forsaken through self-giving love.

In this self-giving love, Christ's sufferings are not only his own but include our sufferings and the sufferings of this time. The cross is the concrete sign that God has bound Godself to the crucified of this world. It is the place where God is once and for all with those who are cast out. For Moltmann, this means there can be no real hope that does not pass through being with the outcast.

From here he moves toward praxis. Hope becomes a way of living that follows the crucified Christ, and the cross contradicts the idea that God sends meaningless suffering. Instead, it shows a God who shares in our suffering and remains present within it. This presence does not remove the suffering, but it gives us the strength to remain human in the middle of it, to resist despair, and to hope beyond what can be seen.

Moltmann names this stance 'protest love': a form of loving resistance that refuses to accept injustice while refusing to stop loving. Hope, in this sense, is grounded in God's own protest against suffering. To follow Christ is to stand with those who suffer and to remember those who bore witness within suffering. Their lives keep open the horizon of God's coming.

Hope, then, is not based on God's distance from suffering but on God's closeness within it; not on denying but on daring to cry *my* God in godforsakenness. The passion of Christ is the very place where hope is born, because it is there that the God who appears to be absent is present as the God who suffers *with and for the world.*

REFERENCES AND BIBLIOGRAPHICAL INFORMATION

Moltmann, J. (1967). *Theology of Hope: On the Ground and the Implications of a Christian Eschatology*. SCM.

Moltmann, J. (1974). *The Crucified God: The Cross of Christ as the Foundation and Criticism of Christian Theology*. SCM.

Moltmann, J. (1975). *The Church in the Power of the Spirit: A Contribution to Messianic Ecclesiology*. SCM.

Moltmann, J. (1981). *The Trinity and the Kingdom: The Doctrine of God*. Harper and Row.

Moltmann, J. (1985). *God in Creation: An Ecological Doctrine of Creation*. SCM.

Moltmann, J. (1990). *The Way of Jesus Christ: Christology in Messianic Dimensions*. SCM.

Moltmann, J. (1993). *The Spirit of Life: A Universal Affirmation*. SCM.

Moltmann, J. (1996). *The Coming of God: Christian Eschatology*. Fortress Press.

Moltmann, J. (2000). *Experiences in Theology: Ways and Forms of Christian Theology*. SCM.

Moltmann, J. (2009). *A Broad Place: An Autobiography*. Fortress Press.

ABOUT THE AUTHOR

Henco van der Westhuizen is associate professor in systematic theology at the University of the Free State, South Africa and consultant for the Faith and Order Commission (World Council of Churches).

JOHANN BAPTIST METZ

Hope from remembrance of suffering

BY ERIK BORGMAN

ARTWORK BY JANWILLEM HOFTIJZER

ABSTRACT

This essay examines Johann Baptist Metz's conviction that authentic hope arises through the memory of those who suffer. For Metz, hope is awakened by remembrance and by a desire for Jesus that disrupts complacency and echoes through culture, calling communities toward compassion and responsibility for one another.

KEYWORDS

memory, suffering, responsibility

BIOGRAPHY

Johann Baptist Metz (1928–2019) was born in 1928 in Bavaria, Germany. At the age of sixteen, he was conscripted into the Wehrmacht. His experiences during World War II gave him memories that would prove foundational for his theology. He was especially stunned by the death of his entire unit, being the only one who had miraculously survived. He became a prisoner of war. Upon returning home, he was bewildered by how widespread the ignorance of the Shoah was.

Hasselaar, Jan Jorrit, Mark van Vuuren, Julieta Matos Castaño, and Erik Borgman, eds. *Voices of Hope: Rediscovering and Building Hope for All.* Amsterdam: Amsterdam University Press / Central European University Press, 2026.

DOI 10.5117/9789048577347-10

Eventually he developed a theology that positioned itself explicitly 'after Auschwitz'.

Metz studied with the Jesuit theologian Karl Rahner (1904–1984), one of the most influential Catholic theologians of the twentieth century. He earned a doctorate in philosophy in 1952 and a doctorate in theology in 1961. In 1954, he was ordained to the priesthood. He became a professor at the Westfälischen Wilhelms Universität in Münster in 1963, where he was director of the Seminar for Fundamental Theology until 1993. Here he developed the theological approach he would come to call '(new) political theology'. Studying with Metz proved transformative for many of his students, who carried on his thinking and commitment in many different contexts. Metz retired from his professorship in Münster in 1993, becoming a visiting professor at the University of Vienna until 1996. He remained active in lecturing and writing until his death in 2019.

Metz was among the founders of the international theological journal *Concilium*, along with Yves Congar (1904–1995), Hans Küng (1928–2021), Karl Rahner, and Edward Schillebeeckx (1914–2009). The journal was established to push forward the development of theology in the wake of the Second Vatican Council. Metz was awarded honorary degrees from the University of Vienna (1994), the Jesuit School of Theology at Berkeley, now part of Santa Clara University (2009), and Heytrop College, London (2013). In 2002, he was awarded the Buber-Rosenzweig Medal for his work in improving Jewish–Christian understanding. To celebrate Metz's seventieth birthday in 1998, a theological conference was organised entitled *Ende der Zeit? Die Provokation der Rede von Gott* [The End of Time: The Provocation of Talking about God]. There was some controversy at this conference due to the prominent role of Cardinal Joseph Ratzinger, the later Pope Benedict XVI (1927–2022). It was common knowledge that Ratzinger was not a friend of Metz's political theology. As archbishop, Ratzinger had blocked the appointment of Metz as professor at the University of Munich, and given that he was the Prefect for the

Congregation for the Doctrine of Faith, many held him responsible for creating the climate in which numerous theologians came into sharp conflict with the Roman Catholic Church's teaching authority. Among these theologians were prominent students of Metz as well as his co-founders of *Concilium*, Hans Küng and Edward Schillebeeckx.

JOHANN BAPTIST METZ ON HOPE

In the early 1970s, Johann Baptist Metz wrote a text entitled *Unsere Hoffnung* [Our Hope]. It was meant to serve as the foundational document for the so-called Würzburg Synod (1971–1975) of the Roman Catholic Church in the Federal Republic of Germany. The purpose of this Synod was to draw conclusions from the Second Vatican Council (1962–1965) for the Western German dioceses. The document was published anonymously, but it was generally known that Metz was its author. Metz returned to the document frequently in later articles. Clearly it was important to him to know that he was not simply venting some personal ideas but that his theology was recognized by the Church as authentic.

In his *Our Hope: Confession of Faith for our Time*, Metz presents a renewed focus on following Jesus Christ as an answer to the burning questions of the moment. The text proclaims that hope for the world is to be found in Jesus, but both the desire for hope and its resonance permeates the general culture. This leads to the conclusion that the Church must neither adapt to the culture nor entrench itself in a one-sided cultural critique. Instead, the task of the Church is to insert itself into society without restraint and without fear of being misunderstood. Misunderstanding will inevitably come the Church's way, as it came to Jesus. The Church will not be granted safety, just as the One in whose footsteps it is called to walk was not granted to go in safety, the document states.

Immediately after the Second Vatican Council, Metz was very open to the cultural changes of the modern era. In the 1970s, however, he engaged in a profound confrontation with the Critical Theory of the so-called Frankfurt School. This brought home to him that modern Enlightenment not only marked empowerment and growth in human freedom but also created new forms of disempowerment and serfdom. On the basis of this dialectical view of the Enlightenment process, Metz elaborated his concept of a political theology as well as of the church, which he saw as 'an institution of social-critical freedom'.

In 1972, in an article for the Dutch-Flemish *Tijdschrift voor Theologie*, Metz distinguished three models of engaging with modern culture. First, there is theology that legitimates the independence of secular thought and reduces the field of which theology can speak with authority to the inner person. Second, there is the tendency to consider modern presuppositions as the norm for what can credibly be thought or said, even within theology. And finally, there is what Metz calls 'an eschatological-political theology' that

> seeks to interpret the surviving forms of Christianity as critically liberating, 'dangerous' memories of freedom and thus to mobilize them within what has been set in motion in the new age of emancipation, secularization and Enlightenment.

The latter indicates what Metz comes to understand as his 'political theology' or the attempt 'to express the eschatological message of Christianity within the relations of the new age as a form of critical-practical thinking'. Ultimately, this led him to the conviction that the credibility of theology depends on its connection to the practical witnessing to hope. It is then that it shows itself to be a genuine 'theology of the world' – as Metz called his own project from the second half of the 1960s onwards – but at the same time as 'exterritoriality opposed to the system', both the functioning societal system and the system of thought that vindicates and justifies it. Ultimately, it prompted Metz to consider memory and narrative as a path to truth, rather than abstract and subject-less thought.

For Metz, the ongoing history of excessive suffering renders implausible not just any belief in linear progress but also any purely argumentative doctrine of salvation. As an alternative, he develops the concept of dangerous memory, arguing that, theologically speaking, hope for the future is born from the memory of suffering, which implies not just a theoretical but also an existential question. The main aim of Metz's 'political theology' is to prevent this question from being overlooked. The heart of his theology is what his assistant of many years, Dominican Tiemo Reiner Peters (1938–2017), called *conversio ad passionem*, or conversion to suffering. For Metz, the core of what he calls *memoria passionis* is the anticipation of a 'future of humanity as a future of those who suffer, the hopeless, the oppressed, the damaged, and the useless of this world'. The refusal to forget their suffering is for Metz both the form and the birthplace of the persistent hope that they will ultimately be included in the redemption of creation that according to the Christian faith is anticipated in the resurrection of Jesus Christ, who suffered and died. As French philosopher and mathematician Blaise Pascal (1623–1662) phrased it: 'Christ will be in agony even to the end of the world. We must not sleep during that time.'

REFERENCES AND BIBLIOGRAPHICAL INFORMATION

Between 2015 and 2018, the collected works of Johann Baptist Metz were published in ten volumes by Herder Verlag. His most important book, *Glaube in Geschichte und Gesellschaft. Studien zu einer praktischen Fundamentaltheologie* (originally published in 1977), is available in English: *Faith in History and Society: Toward a Practical Fundamental Theology*, New York: Crossroad 2007.

Metz, J.B. (1977). *Glaube in Geschichte und Gesellschaft: Studien zu einer praktischen Fundamentaltheologie*. Herder.

Metz, J.B. (2007). *Faith in History and Society: Toward a Practical Fundamental Theology* (J.M. Ashley, Trans.). Crossroad.

Metz, J.B. (n.d.). *Collected Works and Resources*. https://johannbaptistmetz.com/

ABOUT THE AUTHOR

Erik Borgman is a lay Dominican and professor emeritus of public theology at Tilburg University, the Netherlands.

MARTIN LUTHER KING JR.

The infinite complexity of hope

BY JACOB BOUWMAN AND SYLVIA VAN DE BUNT

ARTWORK BY JANWILLEM HOFTIJZER

ABSTRACT

This essay elaborates on Martin Luther King's account of hope growing from civil rights movements, peace, and poverty reduction. Hope sustains nonviolent resistance and confronts systems of oppression and discrimination with conviction. King believed that 'we must accept finite disappointment but never lose infinite hope', a stance that keeps open the possibility of justice.

KEYWORDS

non-violence, justice, infinite

BIOGRAPHY

Martin Luther King Jr. (1929–1968), a Baptist minister and visionary civil rights leader, championed nonviolent resistance to end racial segregation and injustice in the United States of America. His powerful oratory, including his 'I Have a Dream' speech, inspired movements for equality around the world. He remains a symbol of hope, courage, justice, and moral leadership.

Hasselaar, Jan Jorrit, Mark van Vuuren, Julieta Matos Castaño, and Erik Borgman, eds. *Voices of Hope: Rediscovering and Building Hope for All.* Amsterdam: Amsterdam University Press / Central European University Press, 2026.
 DOI 10.5117/9789048577347-11

Between 1955 and 1965, Dr. Martin Luther King Jr. became the face of the civil rights movement in the United States, which non-violently demanded an end to the social inequality resulting from centuries of slavery. He gave many people hope for a more just society. 'We Shall Overcome' is the song sung during the movement's demonstrations and marches that empowered people to set a course of hope for a better future.

He supported Rosa Parks with a bus boycott when she resisted segregation on public transport in late 1955. On 28 August 1963, he delivered his famous 'I Have a Dream' speech in front of 250,000 people in Washington D.C. In 1965, he led the protest marches from Selma to Montgomery for voting rights. He received many honours, including the Nobel Peace Prize (1964) and an honorary doctorate from Vrije Universiteit Amsterdam (1965).

Near the end of his life, he broadened his struggle for social justice, first by speaking out against the Vietnam War and, not long thereafter, becoming involved in the Poor People's Campaign against poverty and unemployment. On 4 April 1967, exactly one year before he was assassinated in Memphis, he gave the speech 'Beyond Vietnam: A Time to Break Silence' at the Riverside Church of the Baptists in New York. He prepared this speech meticulously. And despite the fact that today the lecture is considered one of his most emotional and powerful speeches, it received very bad press at the time. According to *The Washington Post*, the speech was a collection of fabrications based on nothing but fantasy. *Life Magazine* called the lecture a script for Radio Hanoi. *The New York Times* criticized the reckless way in which King had compared American military methods to those of the Nazis. Even his allies in the oldest civil rights movement in the US, the NAACP (National Association for the Advancement of Coloured People), were unpleasantly surprised. They resolutely rejected any attempt to unite the civil rights movement with the peace movement. King denied that he was pushing for this. He believed that everyone had a duty to be active in both the civil rights movement and the peace movement. He had become convinced that these issues had to be addressed together. In 1967, he saw the stagnation, polarization, and violence in the United States and beyond and expressed his calling to 'carve a stone of hope out of a mountain of despair'.

After its initial successes, the civil rights movement ran into difficulties. A white countermovement emerged. The Vietnam War swallowed up the public budget for poverty reduction among the descendants of enslaved people. He saw that supporters were once again becoming bystanders and even opponents of his struggle for a just society. President Johnson was also annoyed with him because of this position. King's advisors warned him not to jeopardize the civil rights movement by joining 'a bunch of bickering, pacifist, socialist hippies'.

But Martin Luther King realized that the hope offered by the successes of the previous period was no longer enough to continue believing in a peaceful advance of social justice. Society was in the grip of war and violence. The old concept of hope no longer worked. He called the new concept of hope that is needed in this situation 'infinite hope'. 'Never lose infinite hope' is a phrase that Dr. King used several times in the spring of 1968.

During this period when he began talking in his speeches about 'never losing infinite hope', he showed symptoms of depression. He drank heavily and slept poorly. His earlier successes failed to give him enough confidence in the renewal of his movement and the improvement of society. He needed more than glimmers of hope. 'Infinite hope' gave his quest a new focus.

MARTIN LUTHER KING ON HOPE

King and the theme of hope are inextricably linked. He used the words 'infinite hope' repeatedly in the last years of his life to keep 'hope' alive. A closer reading shows a layered understanding of hope – one urgently needed in a polarised public debate preoccupied with nationalism and the Vietnam War.

One of the last essays he wrote before he was assassinated on 4 April 1968 was titled *A Testament of Hope*. In it, he elaborated on this concept of infinite hope.

'We must accept finite disappointment but never lose infinite hope' is the full quote he introduced into the public debate in the last months of his life. He had already used the words in 1962 in a sermon on 'Shattered Dreams' based on Bible passages about King David's plans to build a temple in Jerusalem and the Apostle Paul's plans for a trip to Spain. In the sermon, he discussed three possible reactions when your plans are not coming to fruition.

First, you can respond with hatred. Everything and everyone are guilty. Second, you can retreat into your inner world, shutting yourself off from everything and everyone. And third, fatalism can be the answer if what you hope for does not become reality. You can come to believe that there is nothing you can do about it anyway. Or no matter how bad things get, it remains God's will. King rejects all three and then advocates a fourth possibility: 'We must accept our unwanted and unfortunate circumstances and yet cling to a radiant hope. The answer lies in developing the capacity to accept finite disappointment and yet cling to infinite hope.'

For King, infinite hope is clearly a concept with religious roots.

King insists that hope cannot be sustained by isolated successes and defeats. To him, hope depends on at least three interrelated variables: civil rights, peace, and poverty reduction. Fighting against oppression and discrimination also means fighting against imposed meanings and conceptual structures. Hope does not consist solely of bright spots. This is also the message of the Martin Luther King Jr. Center for Nonviolent Social Change: If you want to maintain hope, the social debate must focus on an approach that pays attention to these three interconnected sources. If this does not align with the conventional concept of hope, make it clear to your audience that you have a concept of hope that can continue to motivate courage and resistance, infinitely!

Inspired by Martin Luther King Jr., VU University Amsterdam launched the We Shall Overcome initiative in 2022, including a lecture series for refugee students. The project combines academic orientation with personal mentorship to help students overcome isolation and reconnect with academic life.

REFERENCES AND BIBLIOGRAPHICAL NOTES

Books

Carson, C. (Ed.). (1998). *The Autobiography of Martin Luther King Jr.* Warner Books.

Chenoweth, E., & Stephan, M.J. (2012). *Why Civil Resistance Works: The Strategic Logic of Nonviolent Conflict.* Columbia University Press.

Eig, J. (2023). *King: A Life*. Farrar, Straus and Giroux.

King, M.L., Jr. (1981). *A Gift of Love* (C.S. King, Foreword). Penguin Random House UK.

King, M.L., Jr. (1986). *A Testament of Hope: The Essential Writings and Speeches* (J.M. Washington, Ed.). Harper Collins.

Websites

The King Center, thekingcenter.org

Stanford University Martin Luther King Institute, kinginstitute.stanford.edu

UNESCO Mahatma Gandhi Institute, Youth Programme, mgiep.unesco.org/the-youth-program/

Martin Luther King Lectures, vu.nl/en/about-vu/more-about/martin-luther-king-lecture-vuvereniging

Geheugen van de VU, *'We Shall Overcome. Memories of Martin Luther King Jr.'*

VU, vu.nl/nl/nieuws/2025/archief-vu-amsterdam-op-erfgoedlijst-unesco

https://vu.nl/en/news/2025/unesco-symposium-be-the-change-at-vu-amsterdam > 'From Kuyper to King', including the final report of symposium

ABOUT THE AUTHORS

Jacob Bouwman is a philosopher and programme developer in the Department of University Relations and Fundraising at Vrije Universiteit Amsterdam, the Netherlands.

Sylvia van de Bunt is the UNESCO Chairholder in Cross-Cultural Sustainability and associate professor at the School of Business and Economics, Vrije Universiteit Amsterdam, the Netherlands.

DESMOND TUTU

Hope, suffering, and witness

BY JOHN KLAASEN

ARTWORK BY JANWILLEM HOFTIJZER

ABSTRACT

This essay explores Desmond Tutu's perspective that hope links suffering and freedom by revealing new possibilities within struggle. For Tutu, hope demands commitment and honest confrontation with injustice. It stands in the space between darkness and emerging light, calling people to act with courage.

KEYWORDS

struggle, light, courage

BIOGRAPHY

Desmond Mpilo Tutu (1931–2021) was born on 7 October 1931 to a Xhosa father and Motswana mother. Like the overwhelming majority of black South Africans, he was born under humble circumstances and raised in poverty. After teaching for a short time, Tutu entered the ordained ministry, beginning a lifelong commitment to resistance, justice, freedom, and liberation. Whether it was on the international arena or at home in South Africa, Tutu believed in the goodness of all

Hasselaar, Jan Jorrit, Mark van Vuuren, Julieta Matos Castaño, and Erik Borgman, eds. *Voices of Hope: Rediscovering and Building Hope for All.* Amsterdam: Amsterdam University Press / Central European University Press, 2026.
 DOI 10.5117/9789048577347-12

people and brought people from opposing sides together. This set Tutu apart as one of the most significant proponents of hope.

In 1976, soon after the Soweto uprising in which students and young people protested against the compulsory use of Afrikaans as a medium of instruction, Tutu became bishop of Lesotho. In many ways, this was a turning point in the history of South Africa. After a mere two years, he was called back to South Africa to lead the South African Council of Churches, which placed him at the forefront of the church's resistance against the Nationalist government. A poor boy from a black township, Tutu soon became an international figure and received the Nobel Peace Prize in 1984.

In 1986, Tutu became Archbishop of Cape Town and was quickly nicknamed 'Arch', a testament to his popularity amongst the people of South Africa for his simplicity and humility. After serving as 'Arch' for about a decade, he was appointed chairperson of the South African Truth and Reconciliation Commission set up by President Nelson Mandela. Tutu's funeral was modest and simple, but the magnitude is still felt by South Africans from different backgrounds, beliefs, and cultures. His legacy remains a site of contestation around suffering and hope.

MEETING DESMOND TUTU

On 17 May 2023, Constitution Day in Oslo, Norway, I had lunch with Qystein Tveter, a leading figure in the Lutheran church and Norwegian politics, and his family. It was my first encounter with him and one that will stay with me forever. Qystein, then in his eighties, recounted his experiences with those who became the first government leaders in democratic South Africa, including the late Archbishop Emeritus Desmond Mpilo Tutu.

It was Qystein who supported Tutu's nomination for the Nobel Peace Prize and invited him and his family and friends to celebrate at his home in Oslo when Tutu received the prize. The two of them were close friends and shared a common vision of freedom and justice for all. In a foreword to a book honouring Qystein on his seventieth birthday, Tutu wrote 'Thank you all for the tremendous help you gave us. We are free because you helped us. Tusen takk! God bless you all.' (2007).

My own personal encounter with Tutu was at a discernment retreat for ordained orders in 1993. I found myself in a room alone with Tutu, and even now, when I think about it, I still cannot believe the humility and deep sense of presence that filled the room. During the interview, Tutu asked me why my referees reported that I was 'very political'. As a university student and active member of the church, I never thought of myself that way. My answer was that I simply shared the stories of my fellow students who came from extreme poverty with the members of my church community through homilies, prayer meetings, and, in particular, through organized youth activities. I was later told that Tutu fully supported my application to the ordained ministry.

Tutu's care for each individual, each community, and each society epitomized his ministry, vocation, social political activism, and person. Born into a poor black community and suffering from a life-threatening illness as a child, it is not an understatement to say that Tutu's vocation and calling as a human being and as Archbishop were based on the belief that God created all people and all things good. Tutu's ministry as layperson, deacon, priest, and bishop was beautifully captured by one of his closest friends at his retirement as 'Arch': 'Raised in a humble teacher's home, living in the shadow of the great injustice. [...] Called to labour with God to help God's children become ever more fully human, which is a glorious destiny.' These words took on a particularly powerful resonance in the South Africa where Tutu was about to lead the Truth and Reconciliation Commission.

DESMOND TUTU ON HOPE

For those of us familiar with the narratives of the Truth and Reconciliation Commission, it is no surprise to witness the pain made visible in Tutu's tears, anger, and emotional breakdowns during the hearings. These visible expressions of vulnerability, appearing alongside his ritualistic and symbolic religious attire and gestures, are synonymous with Tutu. The expression of emotions reflected his genuine connection and empathy with the victims of oppression. One always had the sense that there was another side, another stage, another episode to the unfolding stories of the victims: a sense of wholeness, healing, and restoration that was waiting to be unlocked.

The theme of hope was never absent from Tutu's writings, public pronouncements, or actions. Amidst the suffering, pain, poverty, oppression, and opposition, there were possibilities and potential. It was easy to be caught up and even captured by the subjugation, poverty, and violence that prevailed in South Africa at the time. In fact, many people of South Africa believed the country was in danger of falling apart. This was only half of the narrative, and Tutu's commitment to the freedom of the whole nation was by no means a small step towards liberation.

Suffering and freedom were connected by hope. Hope is the interlocutor of two different or opposing phenomena, and it makes the dialogue or dialectic possible within a framework of newness. Tutu, who had suffered under Apartheid laws for most of his life, symbolized the suffering of most South Africans. He demonstrated his understanding of that suffering during the public hearings of the Truth and Reconciliation Commission by allowing himself to be vulnerable and fragile. He exemplified newness within his own vocational journey when he became the first black Archbishop and one of only four South African Nobel Peace Prize winners. Tutu further demonstrated this 'wholeness' in his leadership of the Truth and

Reconciliation Commission, which helped South Africa avert civil war and move from Apartheid to democratic rule.

For Tutu, suffering was intertwined with hope. The intensity, capacity, and commitment that accompany processes of hope almost always encounter suffering at the crossroads of injustices, oppression, domination, and marginalization. There will always be opposition when suffering is confronted because power is always at stake: the power to maintain the status quo, preserve personal gains at all costs, deprive some for the benefit of others, and indulge the few ever more, irrespective of those who are deprived of basic human needs. These are phenomena that symbolize success within the consumerist, capitalist, and competitive worldviews of the twentieth century. Within this tension of suffering and hope, the latter becomes the point of connection for newness, wholeness, and healing. Hope stands between the darkness of the apartheid history and the light that opens up for people, helping them to see again and to reclaim the world they are intended to take responsibility for.

Hope diminishes suffering to its present state: it does not have to be permanent, it does not have to define one's humanity, and it does not have to limit the choices one has. Hope reduces suffering to the genuine pain it causes, whether present or future. Without hope, suffering leaves damaging scars that reduce life to less than the fullness of life for all people and all creatures, human and non-human. It is at this intersection of suffering and the fullness of life that hope resides – lingering and ready to draw us from despair toward our true destiny.

Hope precipitates transformation. War, dehumanization, inequalities, discrimination, and poverty do not define our humanity. These atrocities, caused by those who strive for 'power over' others, do not exist as unchanging. People like Tutu, Qystein, and the victims of Apartheid have the capacity to overcome these dehumanizing acts and help establish a world where all are loved, equal, empowered, and free. It is hope that spurs people and that motivates people and calls on people to take responsibility for the well-being of all people and all creation.

This is what it means to witness, to prophesy, to serve, to empower, to be true to ourselves. It means that our shared humanity invites us to recognize ourselves in the eyes of the other – the stranger, the wanderer, those who are different. When we look in and through their eyes, we witness our own beauty because the eyes of the other reflect the image of who we are in a more complete way. Instead of the restricted self that is limited to the interpretation of an isolated individual, through the eyes of the other, I have a broader vision of the more complete self.

Hope unlocks the call and ultimate vocation to free the other, and in doing so, to free myself. Tutu refers to this process as Ubuntu: 'I am because of you'. During the Truth and Reconciliation Commission, this was embodied in his clerical attire, religious symbols, and rituals, which created liberating moments in the deep spiritual pauses of interruption. These pauses became moments of hope – glimpses of sunrise after a long night of painful testimonies.

Following the example of people like Tutu, we too can become that catalyst of hope that defeats all kinds of despair. We are also empowered through hope to be faithful to the call of peace where there is war, freedom where there is captivity, liberation where people are discriminated against, to feed those who are in poverty and heal those who are sick.

Tutu remains one of the most revered figures across the different cultural and racial groups in South Africa. His own personhood is intertwined with the other, and his calling within the holy orders is at the intersection of suffering and witness. When 'suffering-witness' is reduced to two independent phenomena, it becomes meaningless and can lead to destruction. But with hope as its catalyst and interlocutor, a new process unfolds that makes the future a living, loving, life-giving, and whole-making reality.

Reflecting on Tutu's highly acclaimed book, *Hope and Suffering: Sermons and Speeches*, Mandela said: 'Desmond Tutu shows each of us how to transform our pain and sorrow into hope and confidence in the future.'

REFERENCES AND BIBLIOGRAPHICAL INFORMATION

Bendana, A., Heiene, G., & Jones, J.Y. (Eds). (2007). *Global Justice: The White Man's Burden—Essays on Development and Justice in Honor of Qystein Tveter*. Fagbokforlaget.

Nuttall, M. (2003). *Number Two to Tutu: A Memoir*. Cluster Publications.

Tutu, D. (1983). *Hope and Suffering: Sermons and Speeches*. Skotaville Publishers.

Tutu, D. (2004). *God Has a Dream: A Vision of Hope for our Time*. Rider.

ABOUT THE AUTHOR

John Klaasen is dean of the Faculty of Theology and Religion at the University of the Free State, South Africa.

FRITS GOLDSCHMEDING

Hope as a basis for finding a new economic direction

BY GOVERT BUIJS

ARTWORK BY JANWILLEM HOFTIJZER

ABSTRACT

This essay describes Frits Goldschmeding's view of hope as a compass for renewing economic life. Hope involves looking beyond the simple extrapolation of the present and encouraging a shift in economic practice toward the good. It is manifested in shared norms, respect for others, and a commitment to doing our best in our actions.

KEYWORDS

norms, responsibility, renewal

BIOGRAPHY

Frits Goldschmeding (1933–2024) was an entrepreneur who introduced the idea of flexible manpower to Europe in the late 1950s. He started out very small, bringing his first temporary employee to her job on the back of his own bike. But his business, which was first

---

Hasselaar, Jan Jorrit, Mark van Vuuren, Julieta Matos Castaño, and Erik Borgman, eds. *Voices of Hope: Rediscovering and Building Hope for All.* Amsterdam: Amsterdam University Press / Central European University Press, 2026.
 DOI 10.5117/9789048577347-13

called Uitzendbureau Amstelveen and was later renamed Randstad Uitzendbureau, grew rapidly.

The concept of a staffing company was already known in the United States. At the suggestion of one of his professors, Frits Goldschmeding wrote his Master's thesis on the phenomenon, visiting the US to see how it worked in practice. Back in the Netherlands, he started his own company. Randstad Uitzendbureau grew exponentially over the next 30 years and became a publicly traded company in 1990.

However, a businessman is always more than just a businessman. Frits Goldschmeding was also a husband, a father, a church member, a former student (of Vrije Universiteit Amsterdam), and a professor at Nyenrode Business University. His Protestant upbringing meant a great deal to him personally, making VU Amsterdam, a Christian university at the time, a natural choice. The courses offered by the economics professor Tjalling Pieter van der Kooy (1902–1992) touched Goldschmeding deeply. Strongly influenced by the famous VU philosopher Herman Dooyeweerd (1894–1977), Van der Kooy combined a solid knowledge of and practical experience in economics with a keen sense of the long-term issues raised by economic growth and the emergence of an unlimited mass consumption economy. The focus was on the guiding ideas of the good life. As early as the 1950s, Van der Kooy spoke out against the all-pervasive role of 'efficiency' and 'profitability' at the expense of questions pertaining to social justice and well-being.

As Randstad grew larger, Goldschmeding began to formulate a corporate moral vision, inspired by what he had learned at VU. He eventually founded the Goldschmeding Foundation for Humans, Work and Economy, which aimed to critically rethink and eventually transform the current economy – which was purely driven by shareholder value and profit – into an economy that serves justice and human flourishing for all.

FRITS GOLDSCHMEDING ON HOPE

It may seem odd to include one of the richest businesspeople in the Netherlands in a collection on voices of hope. As so often is the case, Goldschmeding's story is that of starting the right business at the right moment. The booming economy of post-war Netherlands created significant demand for flexible work to accommodate circumstances that were changing by the day. But Goldschmeding refused to simply 'go with the flow'. He thought deeply about the long-term future of his company and later, through the Goldschmeding Foundation, of the economy at large.

Frits Goldschmeding wanted his company to be a long-term force for good in the world. He developed a distinctive corporate vision that focused on three basic principles, which he ultimately set out in Randstad's annual reports. Later he started the Goldschmeding Foundation to promote a new vision of the economy at large, first in the Netherlands and eventually well beyond that. When he started the Foundation, he explicitly stated that it would have a time horizon of at least 100 years. When an economy goes astray, as he felt the modern economy had done both socially and ecologically, one should not be satisfied with small, short-term scratches at the surface. Goldschmeding felt he should aim to develop a long-term course leading toward a new direction.

Goldschmeding's first principle in his corporate vision is adapted from the phrase 'simultaneous realization of norms' coined by his former professor Van der Kooy based on Dooyeweerd's insight that reality is a complex interplay of different irreducible aspects and corresponding types of actions such as matter, life, power, truth, sociality, beauty, efficiency, legality, morality, and religiosity. Reduction is dangerous: when truth becomes a matter of power or financial efficiency, for instance, truth is lost. For the economy, this view implies that human flourishing requires the application of a multidimensional set of indicators and not just GDP or, at the company level, EBITDA. A company only be said to operate well if it at least avoids causing social, ecological, or moral harm, and ideally contributes positively to these dimensions of society. Goldschmeding himself formulated this 'simultaneous realization of norms' as follows: 'A company should be seen as a cooperative undertaking in which simultaneously serving the interests of all direct and indirect stakeholders can guarantee the long-term perspective and continuity of the corporation.'

The second principle of Goldschmeding's corporate vision comes from the Great Commandment in the Bible: 'Love God with all your heart and your neighbour as yourself.' The young Frits had of course picked this up through Bible readings, sermons, and lectures. This general exhortation, however, called for a more concrete instantiation. The best way to interpret and apply this key concept of love of God and neighbour (in Greek: *agape*) was: to know, to serve, and to trust. This led to Randstad's second principle for dealing with clients and stakeholders: 'To know, to serve, to trust is the heart of the moral vision of the company, as an instantiation of love, which is at the heart of morality.'

Goldschmeding's third principle is a tricky one: striving for perfection. When are we justified in calling something perfect? In an imperfect world, the answer is of course never, which means this third principle can be used to constantly criticize employees. But that is certainly not the way Goldschmeding meant it. In a company, everyone should do their very best to know, to serve, and to trust as well as to consider the interests of all stakeholders. But it is not up to the manager or the corporate code to determine what is the best in concrete circumstances. It is crucial to give space to the creativity, the ingenuity, and the resourcefulness of all co-workers. A sloppy attitude, however, undermines this entire endeavour. Striving to do your job well is essential, and accuracy and trustworthiness are key in dealing with clients, as they are signs of respect and yes, even of love. The third principle is thus worded as follows: 'Although we have to acknowledge human imperfection, we may expect from all people involved in the company that they strive for perfection.'

Although Frits Goldschmeding did not explicitly include hope in his basic principles, it is evident throughout his actions and reflections, as we have seen in the above. He felt strongly that the future should not just be an extrapolation of the present but rather something to think about in hope in order to change its course for the better.

REFERENCES AND BIBLIOGRAPHICAL INFORMATION

Goldschmeding Foundation. (n.d.). *Goldschmeding Foundation.* https://goldschmeding.foundation/

Rupert, J., Hengstmengel, J., Haan, R., Goldschmeding, F., van Geest, P., & Commandeur, H. (2016). *Kennen, dienen, vertrouwen: Naar de bronnen van de Goldschmeding Foundation voor mens, werk en economie.* Boom.

ABOUT THE AUTHOR

Govert Buijs is a political philosopher and holds the Frits Goldschmeding Chair for Societal and Economic Renewal at Vrije Universiteit Amsterdam, the Netherlands.

JANE GOODALL

Hope rooted in nature and relationship

BY JULIETA MATOS CASTAÑO

ARTWORK BY JANWILLEM HOFTIJZER

ABSTRACT

This essay reflects on Jane Goodall's understanding of hope as arising from our connection with the natural world and with others. Her scientific insights, faith in young people, and belief in nature's resilience show us that hope is a relational and active choice that helps us protect and reimagine our shared future.

KEYWORDS

nature, relationship, action

BIOGRAPHY

Jane Goodall (1934–2025) was a British primatologist, ethologist, and anthropologist who expanded the way we understand nature and other species. Her research on wild chimpanzees in Gombe Stream National Park, Tanzania revealed that the gap between humans and other animals is far smaller than the Western worldview once assumed.

Hasselaar, Jan Jorrit, Mark van Vuuren, Julieta Matos Castaño, and Erik Borgman, eds. *Voices of Hope: Rediscovering and Building Hope for All.* Amsterdam: Amsterdam University Press / Central European University Press, 2026.
 DOI 10.5117/9789048577347-14

Growing up in wartime England, she spent hours observing birds and seeing life through the eyes of her dog, Rusty, whom she called 'her teacher'. She observed that animals also have inner lives, emotions, thoughts, and personalities. That sense of kinship with the living world became the foundation for all her thinking and actions.

In 1957 Goodall travelled to Kenya, fulfilling a childhood dream of going to Africa. There she met Louis Leakey, a paleoanthropologist and curator of the Coryndon Museum in Nairobi. Jane's patience and observational sensitivity stood out, and Leakey offered her the opportunity to study wild chimpanzees in Gombe.

In 1960 she was a trailblazer: a young woman, guided by curiosity, living alone in the African wilderness and entering a male-dominated world without any formal scientific training. She immediately challenged the objectivity and detachment of Western scientific thought by naming the chimpanzees instead of numbering them. Refusing to see empathy as unscientific, she observed Flo, Fifi, David Greybeard, and others, documenting their emotions and personalities. She saw tenderness, conflict, curiosity, and grief. In doing so, she transformed the field of primatology and what we understand as being human, describing that which defines our humanity as our capacity to recognize ourselves within other beings.

One of her most famous quotes is: 'I'd like to be remembered as someone who really helped people to have a little humility and realize that we are part of the animal kingdom, not separated from it.'

After several years of fieldwork, Goodall became one of the few people to earn a PhD at Cambridge University without an undergraduate degree. In 1977, she founded the Jane Goodall Institute, which supports research, conservation, and community-centred development across Africa and beyond. A decade later, she launched Roots & Shoots, a youth-led movement that is now active in more than 100 countries, inspiring young people to act for animals, people, and the planet.

Goodall was named a UN Messenger of Peace (2002) and has received the Kyoto Prize, the Benjamin Franklin Medal in Life Science, and the Templeton Prize. Until the end of her life, she continued to travel and speak about conservation and the moral imagination we need to create a thriving future.

JANE GOODALL ON HOPE

When we think of Jane Goodall, we see a woman extending her hand to a chimpanzee, a gesture that symbolizes connection and trust. Jane Goodall has been a voice and a *figure* of hope. She invites us to rediscover hope through connection. In a world where dominance and control define our relationship with nature, Goodall offers an alternative grounded in empathy. Her life reminds us that we can and should find hope in our relationships with nonhuman beings and in the act of paying attention to the gaze of an animal or the rustle of leaves.

In *The Book of Hope* (written with Douglas Abrams), Goodall insists that hope is not passive or naive. It is 'a human survival trait'.

> Hope is often misunderstood. People tend to think that it is simply passive wishful thinking: I hope something will happen but I'm not going to do anything about it. This is indeed the opposite of real hope, which requires action and engagement. (Goodall & Abrams, 2021: xviii)

For Goodall, we cultivate hope through our capacity for connection, and she invites us to do the same by looking closely, listening with attention, and meeting the living world with an open hand, just as she did with chimpanzees. 'We are not too late,' Goodall reminds us. Hope is an act of moral imagination to envision a kinder future in which the world heals.

In *The Book of Hope*, Goodall grounds her vision of hope in four pillars. The first one is human intellect. Our intelligence, when guided by empathy and purpose, can become a force for healing. She often warned that intelligence without wisdom leads to harm, and that we must use our intellect for the benefit of all life. For Goodall, hope flourishes when intellect serves compassion instead of domination.

'I think maybe it takes a lot of time in our evolution for us to realize that we can never attain our human potential unless our head and heart work together.' (Goodall & Abrams, 2021: 57)

Her second source of hope relates to the resilience of nature. During her decades in Gombe, she witnessed the regeneration of forests after fire, trees returning to barren hillsides, and animals adapting with incredible tenacity. She saw life persist even after great loss. 'Whenever you give nature a chance,' she says, 'nature returns.'

The third pillar is the power of young people. Youth are the custodians of the planet. The global Roots & Shoots movement began with Tanzanian students who wanted to make a difference. Their actions have inspired thousands across the world. 'Everywhere I go, I meet young people who are making a difference, cleaning rivers, planting trees, helping animals. They will not give up.' (Goodall & Abrams, 2021, p. 115)

Finally, Goodall often spoke of hope as something sustained by the human spirit and the persistence that refuses to give into despair. She saw it in people rebuilding after war, in those protecting endangered species, and in small acts of care that go unnoticed but that keep the world alive. 'It is an ability to deliberately tackle what may seem an impossible task. And not give up even though we know there is a chance we might not succeed.' (Goodall & Abrams, 2021, p. 147)

Together, these four sources form a philosophy of hope that recognizes that the same forces that destroy can also heal when guided by empathy and imagination. For Goodall, hope is both a moral compass and a daily practice to keep the light of possibility alive even when the world is dark.

Goodall's philosophy of hope is relational and grows from our attention to the web that binds all life together. Hope is the practice of seeing and caring. Sadly, many people today have become too disconnected from nature. Living in cities surrounded by concrete and asphalt, we no longer see the stars at night, hear the wind moving through the trees, or wake up to the songs of birds at sunrise.

This disconnection leads to an unfortunate loss of understanding and empathy for nature. In later reflections, Goodall expands on this theme during an interview:

> We must realize that we humans are not separate from the natural world. So many people live in cities and are unaware that we depend on the natural world for everything: food, water and clothing. We rely on healthy ecosystems. But as we continue our selfish development of this materialistic lifestyle, we destroy these ecosystems. We need a new mindset.

In a time marked by ecological grief and uncertainty, Jane Goodall invites us to rediscover hope as commitment. In her last video, released posthumously, Jane Goodall left us with a final message: 'You have it in your power to make a difference. Don't give up. There is a future for you. Do your best while you're still on this beautiful planet Earth that I look down upon from where I am now.'

REFERENCES AND BIBLIOGRAPHICAL INFORMATION

Goodall, J., & Berman, P. (1999). *Reason for Hope: A Spiritual Journey*. Hachette.

Goodall, J., & Abrams, D. (2021). *The Book of Hope: A Survival Guide for Trying Times*. Celadon Books.

Jane Goodall Institute. (n.d.). *Jane Goodall Institute Archives*.

National Geographic. (n.d.). *Jane Goodall Championed Animal Conservation for Six Decades*. https://www.nationalgeographic.com/impact/article/Jane-Goodall-championed-animal-conservation-for-six-decades

ABOUT THE AUTHOR

Julieta Matos Castaño is a research associate at Vrije Universiteit Amsterdam and a practitioner in the field of futures thinking and design at Futures Compass, based in the Netherlands.

POPE FRANCIS

Hope does not disappoint

BY ERIK BORGMAN

ARTWORK BY JANWILLEM HOFTIJZER

ABSTRACT

This essay explores Pope Francis's understanding of hope as both a virtue and a necessity for human life. He urges us to become 'singers of hope' in our daily actions, responding to a world where everything within us and around us cries out for renewal.

KEYWORDS

renewal, virtue, experience

BIOGRAPHY

The man who on 19 March 2013 became Pope Francis was born in 1936 in Buenos Aires, Argentina. His name was Jorge Mario Bergoglio. Both his parents were of Italian descent. He was a chemical engineer before he started studying for the priesthood and entered the Society of Jesus, the Jesuit Order. He was ordained a priest in 1969 and in 1973 was named superior of the Jesuits in Argentina. After that, he was sidelined for a time within his Jesuit community due

Hasselaar, Jan Jorrit, Mark van Vuuren, Julieta Matos Castaño, and Erik Borgman, eds. *Voices of Hope: Rediscovering and Building Hope for All.* Amsterdam: Amsterdam University Press / Central European University Press, 2026.
 DOI 10.5117/9789048577347-15

to tensions in the Argentinian province and what he later acknowledged as policy mistakes. Immediately after his election as pope, rumours circulated that he had been responsible for the kidnapping and torture of two fellow Jesuits during the so-called *Guerra Sucia*, the Dirty War waged by Argentina's military dictatorship against perceived left-wing political opponents. These allegations were later shown to be unfounded.

In 1980, Bergoglio became rector of the Philosophical and Theological Faculty of San Miguel, where he had been a student. Bergoglio became auxiliary bishop of Buenos Aires in 1992 and archbishop in 1998. In 2001 he was appointed cardinal and in 2005, he was elected president of the Argentine Episcopal Conference, a position to which he was re-elected in 2008. During his presidency, Bergoglio issued an apology for the church's failure to protect people from the military junta during the Dirty War.

As an archbishop, Bergoglio was known for his personal humility, his commitment to social justice, and his simple lifestyle: he lived in a small apartment, travelled by public transportation, and cooked his own meals. At the conclave in 2005, the year Joseph Ratzinger became Pope Benedict XVI, Bergoglio was also considered to be a strong candidate. In 2007, Bergoglio had a prominent role at the Fifth Episcopal Conference of Latin America and the Caribbean (CELAM), whose theme was 'Disciples and missionaries of Jesus Christ so that our peoples may have life in Him'. Bergoglio was elected president of the committee drafting the final document. Many things presented in that closing document found their way into the first document he published as Pope Francis in 2013: the apostolic exhortation *Evangelii Gaudium* on the proclamation of the Gospel in today's world.

At the conclave following the resignation of Benedict XVI, Bergoglio was initially considered an outsider. Once elected, he became the first Pope of non-European origin, the first Latin American Pope, and the first Jesuit Pope. He was also the first to take the name Francis, a tribute to Francis of Assisi. It proved to be an indication for the style of his pontificate that before blessing them he asked the crowd on St. Peter's Square to pray for 'the bishop emeritus of Rome' and for the new 'bishop of Rome'. Ever since, wherever he spoke to crowds, he asked them not to forget to pray for him.

Stressing the necessity of reform, Pope Francis had some very outspoken and influential opponents within the hierarchy of the Catholic Church. Francis emphasized what is called 'the preferential option for the poor', indicating that the universality of the church is shown in what it does for those in need and those lacking power. He devoted special attention to migrants and refugees, he strongly condemned violence and war, and praised attempts at reconciliation. In 2015, he wrote *Laudato Si'*, the now famous encyclical on the care for the earth as our common home and how to deal with the ecological crisis. In 2021, he announced the so-called Synodal Process, meant to make all members of the Catholic Church responsible for the course and the mission of the church. Pope Francis died quite unexpectedly on 21 April 2025.

POPE FRANCIS ON HOPE

Once every 25 years, the Roman Catholic Church celebrates a Holy Year, a Jubilee. On Ascension Day 2024, Pope Francis officially announced the Holy Year of 2025. It was to be opened on 24 December 2024 and end on 6 January 2026. The theme of this Jubilee is hope. The Pope wrote in the bull proclaiming the Jubilee that it was his wish that the celebration 'illuminates the light of Christian hope to every man and woman, as a message of God's love addressed to all'.

The bull is entitled *Spes non confundit*, or 'Hope does not disappoint'. The title is taken from the Letter of Saint Paul to the Romans, where it says:

> Since we are justified through faith, we have peace with God through our Lord Jesus Christ, through whom we have obtained access to this grace in which we stand; and we boast in our hope of sharing in the

> glory of God... Hope does not disappoint, because God's love has been poured into our hearts through the Holy Spirit that has been given to us. (Romans 5:1-2 and 5)

According to Catholic teaching, hope is a so-called 'theological' virtue. This means that hope comes from God and is directed to God. Being enduringly present in the life of the Church, the Holy Spirit illuminates believers with the light of hope. Thus, the Holy Spirit is, as the Pope puts it, like an ever-burning lamp, sustaining and invigorating our lives. Pope Francis echoes Saint Paul when he says that Christian hope does not deceive or disappoint because it is grounded in the certainty that nothing can ever separate us from God's love. It is not us but God who sustains hope, Francis stresses: 'Hope is born from love and based on the love springing from the pierced heart of Jesus upon the cross.' Quoting the Apostle Paul again – 'while we were enemies, we were reconciled to God through the death of his Son', and 'more surely, having been reconciled, will we be saved by his life' (Romans 5:19) – Pope Francis argues that the life of Christ becomes manifest in a life of faith that grows in openness to God's grace. It is 'enlivened by a hope constantly renewed and confirmed by the working of the Holy Spirit'.

It is the task of the church to bear faithful witness to this message of hope in every part of the world, according to Francis. In the homily during the pontifical celebration of vespers in which the Holy Year was announced, Francis encouraged the whole church to become 'singers of hope in a culture marked by much despair':

> By our actions, our words, the decisions we make each day, our patient efforts to sow seeds of beauty and kindness wherever we find ourselves, we want to sing of hope, so that its melody can touch the heartstrings of humanity and reawaken in every heart the joy and the courage to embrace life to the full.

Hope is a necessity, according to Francis, but in our time and age it often seems to be sorely lacking:

> Each of us has a need of hope in our lives, at times so weary and wounded, our hearts that thirst for truth, goodness and beauty, and our dreams that no darkness can dispel. Everything, within and outside of us, cries out for hope and continues to seek, even without knowing it, the closeness of God.

Francis is well aware that nobody, including the Catholic Church, has hope available on demand. The Church also has to be given hope,

> so that when she feels wearied by her exertions and burdened by her frailty, she will always remember that, as the Bride of Christ, she is loved with an eternal and faithful love, called to hold high the light of the Gospel, and sent forth to bring to all the fire that Jesus definitely brought to the world.

With a quote from the German-Italian theologian Romano Guardini (1885–1968), on whom he once started a dissertation he never finished, Francis stressed God's faithfulness, particularly in difficult times. Guardini suggested that God may be closer to our age than to other ages because of the precarity of our situation.

In order to experience this divine closeness right here and now, Christians have to continue to faithfully account for the hope that is in them (cf. 1 Peter 3:18). 'What we – all of us – need, ... is hope. Hope does not disappoint: let us never forget this,' Francis stressed.

REFERENCES AND BIBLIOGRAPHICAL INFORMATION

Francis (2024, May 9). *Spes non confundit* [Bull of indiction of the Jubilee of 2025]. Vatican. www.vatican.va/content/francesco/en/bulls/documents/20240509_spes-non-confundit_bolla-giubileo2025.html

Francis (2024, May 9). *Homily during the Pontifical Celebration of Vespers on Ascension Day* [Proclamation of *Spes non confundit*]. Vatican. www.vatican.va/content/francesco/en/homilies/2024/documents/20240509-indizione-giubileo.html

ABOUT THE AUTHOR

Erik Borgman is a lay Dominican and professor emeritus of public theology at Tilburg University, the Netherlands.

VÁCLAV HAVEL

The certainty that something makes sense

BY ERIK BORGMAN

ARTWORK BY JANWILLEM HOFTIJZER

ABSTRACT

This essay examines Václav Havel's understanding of hope as the awareness people carry within themselves of the strength to confront their own powerlessness. Hope reaches beyond immediate experience and is anchored in something higher than us, grounding human responsibility. For Havel, hope calls us to serve the world's openness and help realize its possibilities.

KEYWORDS

meaning, responsibility, possibility

BIOGRAPHY

His definition of hope became world famous. According to the Czech dissident philosopher and playwright – and later politician and president – Václav Havel (1936–2011), hope is not 'the conviction that something will turn out well, but the certainty that some-

Hasselaar, Jan Jorrit, Mark van Vuuren, Julieta Matos Castaño, and Erik Borgman, eds. *Voices of Hope: Rediscovering and Building Hope for All.* Amsterdam: Amsterdam University Press / Central European University Press, 2026.
 DOI 10.5117/9789048577347-16

thing makes sense, regardless of how it turns out'. Being an agnostic, he added:

> It transcends the world that is immediately experienced, and is anchored somewhere beyond its horizons... I feel that its deepest roots are in the transcendental, just as the roots of human responsibility are, though of course I can't – unlike Christians, for instance – say anything about the transcendental.

For quite a while, he had lived more or less on pure hope. Nothing else was available in Czechoslovakia between the late 1960s and late 1980s.

Havel was born in Prague on 5 October 1936 into a wealthy family of real estate developers. His grandfather on his mother's side was a Czechoslovak ambassador and a well-known journalist. In the early 1950s, under Communist rule, Václav Havel became an apprentice in a chemical laboratory and simultaneously took evening classes at a gymnasium. Because of his class background, he was not accepted at any humanities programme after his graduation. He studied at the Faculty of Economics of the Czech Technical University in Prague instead but did not finish his degree. He did his military service from 1957 to 1959 and subsequently found employment as a stagehand, studying dramatic arts by correspondence. In 1963, his first play *The Garden Party* was performed; it immediately won him international acclaim. It was followed by *The Memorandum* and *The Increased Difficulty of Concentration*. After the Warsaw Pact invasion of Czechoslovakia in August 1968, which ended the so-called Prague Spring, Havel's plays could no longer be performed. Forbidden to leave Czechoslovakia, he was unable to see foreign theatre performances.

During the Warsaw Pact invasion, Havel worked for Radio Free Czechoslovakia and subsequently had to take a job at a brewery. His reputation as a dissident was established internationally with the publication of the *Charter 77 Manifesto*, which defended the human rights that the Czechoslovakian government officially endorsed but systematically violated in practice. Having publicly defended the Czech psychedelic rock band The Plastic People of the Universe when they were imprisoned in 1977, Havel co-founded the Committee for the Defence of the Unjustly Prosecuted in 1979. Havel was repeatedly imprisoned, under constant government surveillance, and often questioned by the secret police. He described his longest period of imprisonment from May 1979 to February 1983 in letters to Olga Šplíchalová, his wife since 1964. The letters were later published as a book. In 1986, Havel was awarded the Erasmus Prize.

With others, Havel established the Civic Forum party, which played a major role in the so-called Velvet Revolution that toppled the Communist system in Czechoslovakia in 1989. He was elected president in the first democratic elections in more than 40 years, and after Slovak independence he became the first president of the Czech Republic in 1993; he was re-elected in 1998. After his first wife died in 1998, he married actress Dagmar Havlová (b. 1953). In 2003, after his second term, he resigned, after which he published a few new plays and essays on political-philosophical issues. His memoir of his experience as president, *To the Castle and Back*, was published in 2007. Havel died on the morning of 18 December 2011 at the age of 75.

VÁCLAV HAVEL ON HOPE

Havel's famous definition of hope comes from an interview with writer and fellow *Charter* 77 activist Karel Hvížďala (1941–2011), which was published in 1990 as *Disturbing the Peace*. In the book, Havel reminisces about the time he was willy-nilly a 'dissident'. The position he adopted – relying on hope at a time when nobody expected the Communist regime to change in the foreseeable future – can be traced back to what is likely his most famous essay, written in 1978: 'The Power of the Powerless'. The original plan was to use the essay as the foundation for a collective book on the nature of freedom, with each invited contributor receiving a copy and responding to it. Before the project could be published, however, Havel was arrested and the essay was banned. The text itself, along with several of the responses, circulated separately as samizdat (underground) publications. The essay was published in English in 1985 in an anthology of contributions from various dissidents and intellectuals in the Soviet sphere of influence, also titled *The Power of the Powerless*.

In his essay, Havel famously introduced the example of a greengrocer who displays in his shop window a sign stating: 'Workers of the world, unite!'. What appears as an enthusiastic endorsement of communism is, in fact, an act of submission to the power of the state, as the absence of such a sign would mark disloyalty and invite punishment. In effect, Havel reasons, the greengrocer and his fellow citizens live within a lie. They know it is a lie, but by accepting their lives within it, they confirm the system, fulfil the system, make the system, are the system – which they know is a system of lies. Thus, they become a lie themselves.

However, according to Havel, people always contain 'within themselves the power to remedy their own powerlessness'. As he saw it, power is only effective insofar as citizens are willing to submit to it. By deciding to stop living a lie and start 'to live in truth', taking their own experiences as the foundation of their lives, they automatically withdraw themselves from the culture prescribed by the state. Havel is convinced that oppression is never universal as long as even a single person refuses to give it power over them. This has its price: being prepared to suffer. Havel writes: 'There are times when we must sink to the bottom of our misery to understand truth, just as we must descend to the bottom of a well to see the stars in broad daylight.' This is how we discover the core of hope: that 'certainty that something makes sense, regardless of how it turns out'.

Havel's thinking here is in line with that of his mentor, philosopher Jan Patočka (1907–1977), who died of a heart attack after an 11-hour interrogation by the secret police. Patočka spoke about 'the solidarity of the shaken', those who no longer believe the promises of systems of power, only trusting the convictions deep within themselves that it should be possible to live a truly good life. To remain oriented in life, we need to 'care for the soul', Patočka argued. We have to cultivate our humanity, which exists in both our freedom and our responsibility to be truly and fully human. By caring for the soul and refusing the humiliation of becoming a living lie, we find our way towards living in truth. *Charter 77* was an expression of this 'living in truth', according to Patočka.

Patočka also spoke of 'negative Platonism', a term referring to the awareness that the world – both as a whole and in all its parts – is open to a future that is genuinely new. It is not predetermined that everything must remain as it is, nor is it humanity's fate to submit passively to necessity. At the same time, we cannot liberate ourselves from all that binds us, challenges us, and makes claims upon us. For Patočka, 'negative Platonism' expresses the conviction that there is something higher than ourselves, something to which human existence is inextricably linked and without which the deepest sources of our historical life run dry. We are called to participate in the realization of the truth towards which all that exists aspires. Against this background, Havel spoke of hope as transcending the world immediately before us and as being anchored beyond its visible boundaries, rooted in the transcendental and inseparable from human responsibility. Hope summons us to the responsibility of serving the unfolding openness of the world.

Havel was not satisfied with a transition from what he called post-totalitarian regimes – like the Communist regime in Czechoslovakia – to a parliamentary democracy. We need an 'existential revolution' first. He explained in *The Power of the Powerless*:

> Above all, any existential revolution should provide hope of a moral reconstitution of society, which means a radical renewal of the relationship of human beings to what I have called the 'human order,' which no political order can replace. A new experience of being, a renewed rootedness in the universe, a newly grasped sense of higher responsi-

> bility, a newfound inner relationship to other people and to the human community – these factors clearly indicate the direction in which we must go.

In other words, we must 'care for our souls', allowing ourselves to be transformed into building blocks of a truly democratic society, one in which we are connected non-violently to our fellow human beings and to the universe in which we participate. The political order in the strict sense should support this, Havel insists. 'It would be presumptuous, however, to try to foresee the structural expressions of this new spirit,' Havel warned, 'without that spirit actually being present and without knowing its concrete physiognomy.' As Patočka had already argued, the soul must take precedence.

From the recent histories of democracies – both those emerging from post-totalitarian regimes and those long established – we now know how destructive such a presumption can be. We seem, in fact, to be living amid its consequences today.

REFERENCES AND BIBLIOGRAPHICAL INFORMATION

Keane, J. (2000). *Václav Havel: A Political Tragedy in Six Acts*. Basic Books.

Havel, V. (1985). 'The Power of the Powerless.' In J. Keane (Ed.), *The Power of the Powerless: Citizens against the State in Central-Eastern Europe* (pp. 23–96). Routledge. https://www.nonviolent-conflict.org/wp-content/uploads/1979/01/the-power-of-the-powerless.pdf

Havel, V. (1988). *Letters to Olga: June 1979–September 1983*. Knopf.

Havel, V. (1989). *Disturbing the Peace: A Conversation with Karel Hvížďala*. Faber & Faber.

Patočka, J. (1989). *Philosophy and Selected Writings* (E. Kohák, Ed.). University of Chicago Press.

ABOUT THE AUTHOR

Erik Borgman is a lay Dominican and professor emeritus of public theology at Tilburg University, the Netherlands.

AUDRE GERALDINE LORDE

Hope is where the sun meets the earth

BY EUGENE FORTEIN

ARTWORK BY JANWILLEM HOFTIJZER

ABSTRACT

This essay explores Audre Lorde's understanding of hope as a political and embodied act. By caring for her body and claiming her voice, she created hope for herself and others, modelling resistance rooted in dignity. For Lorde, hope is communal – sustained by shared struggle, solidarity, and a purposeful way of living amid uncertainty.

KEYWORDS

embodiment, dignity, solidarity

'Where the sun meets the earth, I will one day stand
and hope will call my name'

BIOGRAPHY

Audre Geraldine Lorde (1934–1992) was born in New York on 18 February 1934. She was a self-described 'black, lesbian, mother, warrior, poet' who devoted her life and creative career to confronting the injustices of racism, sexism, classism, and homophobia. Born to West

Hasselaar, Jan Jorrit, Mark van Vuuren, Julieta Matos Castaño, and Erik Borgman, eds. *Voices of Hope: Rediscovering and Building Hope for All.* Amsterdam: Amsterdam University Press / Central European University Press, 2026.
 DOI 10.5117/9789048577347-17

Indian immigrant parents, she attended Catholic schools and published her first poem, 'Seventeen', while still attending Hunter High School. She obtained her Bachelor's degree from Hunter College.

Lorde married Edwin Rollins, a white gay man, with whom she had two children. The marriage ended in 1970. In 1972, Lorde met her lifelong partner, Frances Clayton. She began teaching at Tougaloo College in 1968. Her teaching experience and her position as a Black queer woman in white academia defined her future life and work. Lorde's work was rooted in her personal experiences – which she used to inform her political objectives – as well as her contributions to feminist theory, race theory, and critical race studies. Lorde's early work, *The Master's Tools Will Not Dismantle the Master's House*, designated the intersections of race, class, and gender.

Lorde published regularly throughout the 1970s and 1980s. It was during this time that she became a civil rights activist as well as an anti-war and women's rights activist. These themes are strongly featured in her poems and other works from that period, such as *Cables to Rage* (1970), *The Black Unicorn* (1978), *Sister Outsider* (1984), and the fictionalised memoir *Zami: A New Spelling of My Name* (1982).

The diagnosis of breast cancer in 1977 and liver cancer six years later profoundly impacted Lorde's work from that point on. She declined surgery and a biopsy, opting to live the rest of her life with a sense of purpose. It was during the period of dealing with the prognosis and the consequent mastectomy that she discovered that there were no publications related to being black and lesbian. Her condition led her to poetically journal her journey with cancer and mastectomy, which was published as *The Cancer Journals* (1980). Through her own voice – her grief, resistance, and courage – Lorde offers hope to those facing their own diagnoses. Her words give strength to women living with cancer, helping them to transform their struggle into hope.

AUDRE LORDE ON HOPE

Audre Lorde's *A Burst of Light* (2017) perhaps best reveals her thoughts on hope while living with cancer as a Black and queer woman. Even though the word 'hope' is not explicitly mentioned, it is a strong underlying theme. The book reveals that, even at a very challenging time in her life, hope for Lorde remained deeply political, embodied, and communal. It was hope that sustained her journey with cancer. Hope, for her, embodied many things. One of these is survival. Even when confronted with a terminal diagnosis, she refused to give in to despair. Even in the presence of fear, she stated, 'I am listening to what fear teaches. I will never be gone. I am a scar, a report from the frontlines, a talisman, a resurrection' (Lorde 2017, p. 51). Here, she does not wish away her fear but rather transforms it into hope, which sustains her on the journey. She writes, 'I know I can broaden the definition of winning to the point where I can't lose' (Lorde 2017, p. 53). Winning, for her, does not necessarily mean defeating the illness but rather living with it on her own terms and by her own choices.

A renowned phrase from the book is 'caring for myself is not self-indulgence, it is self-preservation, and that is an act of political warfare' (Lorde 2017, p. 130). This statement is crucial to Lorde's framing of hope, that taking care of her body is a profoundly political act. In a society where Black and queer women are marginalized, her self-care is a form of resistance and refusal, creating hope for herself and others. Her resistance becomes a source of hope and inspiration, indicating that her life has value and is worth fighting for.

Lorde's confrontation with her own mortality and the uncertainty of her ailing health is perhaps the most inspiring part of her story of hope. As her condition worsened, she continued to live with purpose and hope. She writes: 'learning not to crumple before these uncertainties fuels my resolve to print myself upon the texture of each day fully rather than forever' (Lorde 2017, p. 126). This statement suggests that her hope is directed towards living in the present with purpose rather than focusing on longevity.

Lorde may have experienced the deterioration caused by cancer on a deeply personal level, but her struggle was never lived in isolation. Her hope, therefore, is not individual but communal. Throughout *A Burst of Light*, she links her own fight for survival to the struggles of Black, queer, and marginalized women, politically and otherwise. Her experience becomes a source of hope rooted in collective resistance. In confronting her illness, she stands in solidarity with women in their own battles – not by offering easy victories but by embodying a hope that persists and resists.

Ultimately, journaling her journey with cancer became a hopeful act for Lorde. She employed her creative writing both to confront her fear and inspire others. She passionately wrote: 'I am going to write fire until it comes out my ears, my eyes, my nose holes – everywhere. Until it's every breath I breathe' (Lorde 2017, p. 71). Today, her work serves as a form of immortality, reverberating to inspire marginalized women far beyond her lifespan.

REFERENCE AND BIBLIOGRAPHICAL INFORMATION

Lorde, A. (1970). *Cables to Rage*. Broadside Press.
Lorde, A. (1978). *The Black Unicorn*. W.W. Norton & Company.
Lorde, A. (1980). *The Cancer Journals*. Aunt Lute Books.
Lorde, A. (1982). *Zami: A New Spelling of My Name*. Crossing Press.
Lorde, A. (1984). *Sister Outsider: Essays and Speeches*. Crossing Press.
Lorde, A. (2017). *A Burst of Light: And Other Essays*. Ixia Press.

ABOUT THE AUTHOR

Eugene Fortein is senior lecturer in church history and church polity at the Faculty of Theology and Religion, University of the Free State, South Africa.

ECUMENICAL PATRIARCH BARTHOLOMEW

The hope of transforming the world

BY JAN JORRIT HASSELAAR

EDITED BY JOHN CHRYSSAVGIS

ARTWORK BY JANWILLEM HOFTIJZER

ABSTRACT

This essay explores Ecumenical Patriarch Bartholomew's view of hope as an expression of faith in the world's transformation and a gift entrusted to future generations. His vision links hope to ecological responsibility and the weaving together of communities, seeking a light capable of shining brighter than the darkness that surrounds us.

KEYWORDS

transformation, ecology, community

BIOGRAPHY

Ecumenical Patriarch Bartholomew has played a prominent and pioneering role in the relationship between religion and environmental issues. As a result of this commitment, the former US Vice President Al Gore nicknamed him the 'Green Patriarch'. In 2008, the Patriarch was named by *Time Magazine* as one of the 100 most influential people for 'defining environmental issues as a spiritual responsibility'. Pope

Hasselaar, Jan Jorrit, Mark van Vuuren, Julieta Matos Castaño, and Erik Borgman, eds. *Voices of Hope: Rediscovering and Building Hope for All.* Amsterdam: Amsterdam University Press / Central European University Press, 2026.
 DOI 10.5117/9789048577347-18

Francis acknowledged and highlighted Ecumenical Patriarch Bartholomew in his encyclical *Laudato Si'* (2015): 'I would mention the statements made by the beloved Ecumenical Patriarch Bartholomew, with whom we share the hope of full ecclesial communion'. And on 28 November 2025, Pope Leo XIV and Ecumenical Patriarch Bartholomew made a joint pilgrimage to Nicaea (today's İznik, Turkey) to mark the 1,700th anniversary of the First Ecumenical Council of Nicaea.

Patriarch Bartholomew was born on 29 February 1940 as Dimitrios Archondonis on the island of Imvros (today's Gökçeada, Turkey). He grew up in a family of four children. During summer holidays, Dimitrios helped in his father's café. From a young age, he also assisted at the altar. In 1961, he graduated cum laude from the Patriarchal Theological School of Halki. He pursued graduate studies at the Pontifical Oriental Institute of the Gregorian University in Rome (Italy), the Ecumenical Institute in Bossey (Switzerland), and the University of Munich (Germany). His doctoral dissertation was submitted to the University of Athens (Greece). Ordained to the Diaconate in 1961 and to the Priesthood in 1969, he served as Assistant Dean at the Theological School of Halki (1968–72) before being appointed as Personal Secretary to the late Ecumenical Patriarch Demetrios (1972–90). He was elected Metropolitan of Philadelphia in 1973 and, subsequently, Metropolitan of Chalcedon in 1990. Since 1975, he has been a member of the Faith and Order Commission of the World Council of Churches and held the position of vice president for eight years prior to his election as Ecumenical Patriarch.

Bartholomew was installed in 1991 as the 270th Archbishop of the Church founded by Andrew the Apostle. Since then, he has served as Ecumenical Patriarch and Archbishop of Constantinople-New Rome. He is primus inter pares among the leaders of the Autocephalous Orthodox Churches, which number approximately 300 million members worldwide. Ecumenical Patriarch Bartholomew is the longest serving Primate of the Apostolic See of Constantinople.

The Patriarch holds numerous honorary doctorates and has received many international awards, including most recently the Templeton Prize (2025) for 'his pioneering efforts to bridge scientific and spiritual understandings of humanity's relationship with the natural world, bringing together people of different faiths to heed a call for stewardship of creation'.

ECUMENICAL PATRIARCH BARTHOLOMEW ON HOPE

In *Encountering the Mystery* (2008), Ecumenical Patriarch Bartholomew describes hope as the greatest gift that

> we have to offer to our children: that we believe and hope in a better world where war is no more, where races and religions are equally respected, where the diversity of nature is celebrated, where all people have enough, and where the language of tolerance is the mother tongue of the global family in order that the God of love may be glorified.

The Patriarch's understanding of hope has profound spiritual roots. In Orthodox spirituality, the message of the kingdom of God is one of hope. This message is not a way of escaping reality but an articulation of the faith in the transformation of this world. The role of the Church is not to conform to this world but to transform the world, to highlight another way of seeing, living, and behaving. Patriarch Bartholomew insists that there is only one way that we shall prevail as individuals and communities of transformation: together.

Ecology is one of the themes at the heart of the Patriarch's ministry, which seeks to transform the world. The core of his ecological contribution lies in the belief that the response to current issues cannot be purely technological. He emphasizes that the response to ecological issues can only be successful if it involves a fundamental and radical change in underlying values and spiritual attitudes. This change is about a transformation from a mindset that takes little or no account of the natural environment and related social issues to a mindset of assuming responsibility for a shared earth.

Ecumenical Patriarch Bartholomew has taken the lead among all religious leaders in his concern for the environment. He is convinced that environmental challenges must be resolved in dialogue and partnership with other religious faiths and scientific disciplines. This conviction led him to establish the Religious and Scientific Committee (1994), which has hosted nine international, interreligious, and interdisciplinary symposia reflecting on the fate of our seas and rivers: the Mediterranean (1995), the Black Sea (1997), the Danube (1999), the Adriatic (2002), the Baltic Sea (2003), the Amazon (2006), the Arctic Sea (2007), the Mississippi River (2009), and the Saronic Islands of Greece (2018). Often held under the joint auspices of the President of the European Commission or the Secretary-General of the United Nations, these symposia have accelerated the pace of religious debate on climate change. Drawing on the symbolism behind his sea-borne symposia, the Patriarch likes to say: 'We are all in the same boat.'

In 2012, the Ecumenical Patriarch decided to focus on smaller meetings, inviting scholars, specialists, and leaders to address targeted issues related to the environment. The first Halki Summit (2012) discussed sustainability; the second, in 2015, explored literature and the arts; the third (2019) examined theological formation; the fourth (2021) looked at living with and learning from the pandemic; the fifth (2022) was about sustaining the future of the planet together and focused on the prophetic ministry of Pope Francis and Ecumenical Patriarch Bartholomew; the sixth (2024) had as its theme 'Water: Spirit and Science'; and the seventh (2027) is about nurturing the soul and the soil.

All these international, interreligious, and interdisciplinary symposia and summits reflect the Patriarch's theological conviction that these issues can only be resolved through close cooperation between governments, business, academia, the arts, media, youth, NGOs, and religions. The distinctive role that the Orthodox Church plays in this is not only to provide a broader perspective but also to add an attitude of gratitude and community (namely, a eucharistic ethos) and simplicity (namely, an ascetic ethos) to the conversation. The eucharistic ethos understands the world not as something to be consumed but rather to be transformed and sanctified. The ascetic ethos focuses on living simply rather than simply living. It means moving away from what we want as individuals to what the world needs as a whole. And a third characteristic ingredient of Orthodox spirituality is joyful sorrow, a sentiment that combines the struggle to reconcile God's light with the darkness that fills the world. Joyful sorrow expresses the conviction that God's light is brighter than any darkness in the world.

At the end of *Encountering the Mystery*, Ecumenical Patriarch Bartholomew cites the third-century Church Father Clement of Alexandria:

> If you do not hope,
> you will never discover
> what lies beyond your hopes.

Ultimately, Ecumenical Patriarch Bartholomew encourages his audience to be unafraid and to contribute to hope by transforming the world through love.

REFERENCE AND BIBLIOGRAPHICAL INFORMATION

Bartholomew I. (2008). *Encountering the Mystery: Understanding Orthodox Christianity Today*. Doubleday.

Chryssavgis, J. (2010). *In the World, Yet Not of the World: Social and Global Initiatives of Ecumenical Patriarch Bartholomew*. Fordham University Press.

Chryssavgis, J. (2016). *Bartholomew: Apostle and Visionary*. Thomas Nelson.

Ecumenical Patriarchate. (n.d.). *Ecumenical Patriarchate of Constantinople*: https://www.patriarchateofconstantinople.com/index.html

ABOUT THE AUTHOR AND EDITOR

Jan Jorrit Hasselaar, economist and theologian, is associate professor of public theology and director of the Amsterdam Centre for Religion & Sustainable Development at Vrije Universiteit Amsterdam, the Netherlands. He is a research fellow at the University of the Free State, South Africa. Jan Jorrit is co-chair of the Global Network for Public Theology.

John Chryssavgis is archdeacon of the Ecumenical Patriarchate and executive director of the Huffington Ecumenical Institute at Hellenic College Holy Cross, the United States.

JOHN D. CAPUTO

Hoping against hope

BY CALVIN ULLRICH

ARTWORK BY JANWILLEM HOFTIJZER

ABSTRACT

This essay explores John Caputo's sense of hope as a happening; an open-ended event that signals how the world might be otherwise. Such hope lives in uncertainty and is realized only when we respond to what calls upon us, human or nonhuman. For Caputo, hope requires radical openness to unexpected possibilities rather than submission to a coercive power.

KEYWORDS

uncertainty, event, openness

BIOGRAPHY

John D. Caputo (b. 1940) was born in Philadelphia, Pennsylvania and grew up in the conservative Catholic world of the pre–Vatican II era. Young and impressionable, the importance of religious devotion and piety led him to begin his novitiate with the Catholic Order, Brothers De LaSalle. He spent three years in formation but found himself in disagreement with his monastic superiors, who regarded his desire

Hasselaar, Jan Jorrit, Mark van Vuuren, Julieta Matos Castaño, and Erik Borgman, eds. *Voices of Hope: Rediscovering and Building Hope for All.* Amsterdam: Amsterdam University Press / Central European University Press, 2026.
 DOI 10.5117/9789048577347-19

to study and teach philosophy as a departure from his religious vocation. In an early display of irreverence, Caputo ignored his superiors' advice and enrolled in a Master's course at Villanova University, after which he obtained a doctorate from Bryn Mawr College in 1968 on Heidegger and Aquinas.

Caputo subsequently taught philosophy at Villanova University in Pennsylvania for the next thirty-six years, holding the David R. Cook Chair for Philosophy and organizing the widely regarded *Religion and Postmodernism* conferences from 1997 to 2003. He retired early in 2004 to become the Thomas J. Watson Professor of Religion and Humanities and Professor of Philosophy at Syracuse University in New York. His formal retirement began in 2011, yet he remains prolific in his writing.

Caputo is most well-known for his religious reading of the French philosopher Jacques Derrida. However, his philosophical and theological expertise also includes the writings of Saint Augustine, Thomas Aquinas, and Meister Eckhart as well as Kierkegaard, Nietzsche, and Heidegger. Caputo's work can be considered through a number of distinct phases, from the more erudite and formulaic nature of his early academic material to the accessible flair and jocularity of some of his later theological texts.

Caputo's approach in terms of theology can be described as 'radical theology', an influential field that his writing has significantly shaped. His fundamental insight – though more sophisticated in its formulation – is that through the lens of Derridean deconstruction, religion or Christianity harbours within itself a non-realisable kernel, desire, or promise for the wholly Other. For Caputo, this kernel – what he calls an 'event' – is profoundly religious, or at least religious in its structure, since it reaches the heart of religious expectation, the 'hope' for a new ordering of the world's very being. Crucially, however, the energy and vitality that generates this hope and keeps it alive is only made possible by acknowledging that its arrival is without any assurance.

JOHN D. CAPUTO ON HOPE

We know from the Jesus traditions in the New Testament – as well as from the context of the Roman Empire in which the Apostle Paul wrote – that the 'logic of hope' refers to a double gesture: not only does hope emerge against all odds but it challenges the other false hopes on offer. Paul's famous passage from Romans 4:18 describes Abraham as 'hoping against hope' not only that he would ostensibly be a 'father of nations' but also to proclaim a different logic of hope based on the affirmation that newness and wholeness would emerge from the margins, without the guarantee of power that follows the logic of empire. Unfurling this alternative 'hoping against hope', in some ways, signals the entire project of Caputo's philosophy of religion and radical theology.

Caputo is interested in questioning any form of assumed power – the powers of religion, Christianity, even the powers of thought itself – not so that nothing will be left in their wake but to allow the promise of a new hope to emerge. One can find this elaborated throughout Caputo's oeuvre particularly in philosophical terms, but in his highly readable semi-autobiographic text, *Hoping Against Hope: Confessions of a Postmodern Pilgrim* (2015), we get a series of snapshots of this quasi-anarchic project. For Caputo, radical theology begins from rejecting the 'master signifier' *par excellence*: the doctrine of an all-powerful, unmoved God. Crucially, as he writes, 'God will not go away, not because God is a necessary being but because God is contingent, a part of the world I have inherited' (178). This means, for Caputo, digging into the roots (*radix* – radical) of theology to get at that energetic principle that animates it.

This 'principle', however, is only half the story, because if theology promises that it is God who is the source of this energy that governs, sustains, and indeed renews all things, Caputo will answer that even 'God' is just a name for something else attempting to get itself expressed – something ultimately unknowable because it is no-thing at all, and yet no less evocative. In Caputo's text *Hoping Against Hope*, as elsewhere in his writing, this 'something else' is what he calls an 'event', a happening that is not the same as an actual thing, entity, or occurrence. An event is a radical in-breaking into the present, a structure of futural expectation to which we respond in obligation and to which we bear witness, not because of its overwhelming presence or powerfulness but because of its 'weak' calling. As another name for hope, then, this 'happening' is not the guarantee that things will turn out for the better, that God will make all things well; instead, it refers to an open-endedness that bears witness to a future possibility of the way things could be otherwise (or not). This open-endedness or uncertainty about the future — poetically captured, for Caputo, in Paul's words about 'the *weakness of God*' on the Cross —functions to relativize the false hopes on offer in the present.

But here Caputo goes even further, for if the sign of the cross confounds the logic of the world through the demonstration of what we might call 'kenotic hope', this is also not a reason to resign oneself to meaninglessness, to the idea that no hope exists at all. Indeed, Caputo's radical suggestion is that 'resurrection' in this context is often misunderstood as a kind of divine bait-and-switch, where God swoops in to clutch victory from the jaws of defeat. For Caputo, such a reading in fact closes down the kenotic hope that calls from God's death on the cross. Instead of knowing how the story ends – that the scales of justice will ultimately be balanced – Caputo insists that true hope can only be realised to the extent that we respond to the call of what calls upon us; to the demand to attend to the stranger – human or non-human – but clearly not as a response to a coercive power. This radical openness or radical hope for a different possibility of the world is predicated on the equal possibility that such openness to the other may prove to be dangerous.

For Caputo, it is precisely this 'undecidability', or radical 'openness', that is the character of the hope we should seek to recover. Hope in this sense – to 'hope against hope' – is not a passive resignation but a bearing witness to a weak call kenotically expressed, which obliges us to get 'justice done'. Radical hope, therefore, is the work of justice, forgiveness, and hospitality, never fully *disclosed* to us in the present but therefore never fully *foreclosed* to us here and now either. To put this another way, it is this impossibility of knowing how things will turn out that becomes the 'quasi-condition' of keeping hope and possibility alive, open for re-imagining, re-formulating, re-incarnating, and renewing.

REFERENCES AND BIBLIOGRAPHICAL INFORMATION

Caputo, J.D. (2006). *The Weakness of God: A Theology of Event*. Indiana University Press.

Caputo, J.D. (2015). *Hoping against Hope: Confessions of a Postmodern Pilgrim*. Fortress Press.

Ullrich, C.D. (2021). *Sovereignty and Event: The Political in John D. Caputo's Radical Theology*. Mohr Siebeck.

Ullrich, C.D. (2022). *Caputo on Radical Political Theology* (Temple Continental: Philosophers for Our Time, Book IV). William Temple Foundation. https://williamtemplefoundation.org.uk/temple-tracts/temple-continental/

ABOUT THE AUTHOR

Calvin D. Ullrich is senior lecturer in interdisciplinary theology and director of the Centre for Interdisciplinary Research in Religion, Community, and Ecologies (CIRRCE) at the University of the Free State, South Africa.

CHARLES SNYDER

Hope as a positive motivational state

BY ERNST BOHLMEIJER

ARTWORK BY JANWILLEM HOFTIJZER

ABSTRACT

This essay outlines Charles Snyder's definition of hope as a positive motivational state grounded in thinking in pathways and a sense of agency. For Snyder, motivation and agency work together to move a person toward desired goals. His hope theory demonstrates how psychological interventions can strengthen these capacities and foster a hopeful outlook.

KEYWORDS

agency, pathways, motivation

BIOGRAPHY

Charles Richard Snyder (1944–2006) was a prominent American psychologist. He is best known for developing what he coined hope theory. Born in 1944, Snyder dedicated his career to exploring human motivation and the emerging field of positive psychology. He earned his PhD in psychology from the University of Kansas, where he later became a professor of psychology.

Hasselaar, Jan Jorrit, Mark van Vuuren, Julieta Matos Castaño, and Erik Borgman, eds. *Voices of Hope: Rediscovering and Building Hope for All.* Amsterdam: Amsterdam University Press / Central European University Press, 2026.
 DOI 10.5117/9789048577347-20

An influential figure in the positive psychology movement, Snyder played a key role in shaping the field's early development. Together with Shane Lopez, he edited the *Handbook of Positive Psychology* in 2002, which offered the first comprehensive global overview of theories and applications within positive psychology. Snyder's work has had a significant impact across various disciplines, including clinical psychology, counselling, and education. Among his most influential publications is *The Psychology of Hope* (1994), a widely cited book that continues to shape our understanding of goal setting, motivation, and well-being.

Snyder conducted extensive research on the nature of hope, demonstrating that individuals with higher levels of hope are more likely to achieve their goals and enjoy greater psychological well-being. Working within a positivistic-empirical research framework, Snyder developed several psychological instruments to measure hope, including the state hope scale and the adult hope scale. Sample items from the state hope scale include: 'I can think of many ways to reach my current goals' and 'At this time, I am meeting the goals that I have set for myself.' Numerous studies using these scales have demonstrated that higher levels of hope are linked to positive functioning across a wide range of life domains. These include improved academic performance and problem-solving abilities, enhanced immune functioning and faster recovery from illness, a reduced risk of depression, increased resilience among trauma survivors, higher levels of relationship satisfaction, better workplace performance and job satisfaction, and lower risk of anxiety among children and adolescents. Hope has also been found to correlate positively with pro-social behaviours such as seeking social support, exhibiting altruism, becoming involved with the community, and helping others.

While it obviously does not offer a deep existential analysis of the human condition, hope theory demonstrates its applicability to everyday goal-setting practices, which can be learned and developed over time. The theory also provides a useful lens for understanding a wide range of phenomena, including relapse prevention, success in sports, and the influence of religious beliefs and practices on health and adaptive coping.

CHARLES SNYDER ON HOPE

Snyder defined hope as a positive motivational state resulting from a cognitive process. This motivational state is based on a sense that successful pathways exist (leading to planning to meet goals) as well as successful agency (i.e. goal-directed energy to use the pathways).

Agency refers to the motivational aspect of hope, the individual's perceived capacity to initiate and sustain movement toward their desired goals. Agentic thinking reflects self-referential thoughts about both starting and continuing progress along a chosen path. This motivational energy is particularly crucial when individuals or groups face obstacles. In such situations, agency fuels the determination needed to pursue alternative strategies and maintain momentum. Pathways thinking represents the perceived ability to generate viable routes toward goal attainment. High-hope individuals or groups tend to believe they can effectively create and navigate multiple pathways, particularly when encountering setbacks. The ability to identify alternative strategies reinforces resilience and adaptability.

For hope to thrive, Snyder believed that goals had to strike a balance: there had to be a degree of uncertainty while remaining realistically attainable. He emphasized the importance of setting intermediate goals and celebrating small successes, which help reinforce both agentic thinking and pathways thinking. Incremental achievements sustain motivation and foster a sense of progress, which in turn enhances overall hope. High-hope people are inclined to be more process-oriented. The process itself is experienced as meaningful. Snyder writes: 'Even if the ultimate goal is out of reach, high-hope people may enjoy and reap psychological benefits from the goal pursuit process.'

Snyder showed a strong interest in the practical application of hope theory in therapeutic and coaching contexts. He developed hope therapy, a psychological intervention aimed at fostering and strengthening a person's sense of hope. This approach helps individuals identify meaningful goals, develop actionable strategies to achieve them, and build confidence in their ability to succeed even when facing significant challenges. Hope therapy is commonly used in counselling individuals dealing with depression, anxiety, trauma, and chronic illness.

Snyder was also interested in examining various life phenomena through the lens of his hope theory. One such example is religious practice. In 2002, he reflected on a collection of papers exploring the impact of religion on health and coping with illness and other life events. He argued that every religion encompasses a 'matrix of goals, pathways for accomplishing those goals, and agency thoughts for applying those pathways'. According to Snyder, most Western religious traditions share six broad categories of ultimate goals: (1) unity, harmony, or relationship with the divine; (2) supernatural assistance in leading a peaceful life; (3) a place in heaven or an equivalent afterlife; (4) social support; (5) an understanding of truth; (6) a deeper sense of life purpose. Concrete activities such as reading sacred texts, participating in rituals, or practicing virtues can be viewed as smaller, more concrete objectives that serve these larger, ultimate goals. Seemingly secular goals – such as helping someone in need – can be linked to these broader, more abstract religious aims. In this sense, many personal goals may take on a sense of sacredness when viewed through a religious or spiritual lens.

A key concept for Snyder here is goal integration, which refers to the degree to which personal goals are aligned with and supportive of each other. Seen through the lens of hope theory, goal integration is a major factor in the impact of religion on well-being. Conflicts between goals are a common human experience, and they are generally associated with reduced psychological well-being. The extent to which a person's religious strivings are harmoniously integrated with their other life goals can therefore have a significant influence on mental health and adaptive functioning.

Snyder also discusses the work of Kenneth Pargament, who identified three religious coping styles. These styles differ in terms of how individuals assign control between themselves and a divine power when facing stress. The first style is a self-directive approach: individuals believe that God has given them the tools (e.g., intelligence, strength, or resources) to manage situations independently. The second style is a collaborative approach: the individual works *with* God in a kind of partnership to address life's challenges. The third style is a deferring approach: control is handed over entirely to God, with the person waiting passively for divine intervention. Pargament's research showed that the self-directive and collaborative approaches are associated with a stronger sense of control and more effective coping. This finding aligns well with hope theory. Individuals using these approaches are often 'high hopers': people who can generate multiple pathways toward their goals and maintain a strong sense of agency. In contrast, those who rely primarily on deferring tend to produce fewer pathways and are generally less proactive in overcoming obstacles.

REFERENCES AND BIBLIOGRAPHICAL INFORMATION

Schornick, Z., Ellis, N., Ray, E., Snyder, B.-J., & Thomas, K. (2023). 'Hope that Benefits Others: A Systematic Literature Review of Hope Theory and Prosocial Outcomes.' *International Journal of Applied Positive Psychology,* 8, 37–61.

Snyder, C.R., Ilardi, S.S., Cheavens, J., Michael, S.T., Yamhure, L., & Sympson, S. (2000). 'The Role of Hope in Cognitive-Behavior Therapies.' *Cognitive Therapy and Research,* 24, 747–762.

Snyder, C.R., Rand, K.L., & Sigmon, D.R. (2002a). 'Hope Theory: A Member of the Positive Psychology Family.' In C.R. Snyder & S.J. Lopez (Eds.), *Handbook of Positive Psychology* (pp. 257–276). Oxford University Press.

Snyder, C.R., Sigmon, D.R., & Feldman, D.B. (2002b). 'Hope for the Sacred and Vice Versa: Positive Goal-Directed Thinking and Religion.' *Psychological Inquiry,* 13, 234–238.

Snyder, C.R., Rand, K.L., King, E.A., Feldman, D.B., & Woodward, J.T. (2002c). 'False Hope.' *Journal of Clinical Psychology,* 58, 1003–1022.

ABOUT THE AUTHOR

Ernst Bohlmeijer is professor of mental health promotion at the University of Twente, the Netherlands.

ALLAN BOESAK

Hope and the language of life in faith and politics

BY MARIUS LOUW

ARTWORK BY JANWILLEM HOFTIJZER

ABSTRACT

This essay explores Allan Boesak's understanding of hope as a new language shaped by the dream of justice, peace, and wholeness. Nurtured by trust, hope draws people into the ongoing struggle against injustice. For Boesak, hope becomes real only when we accept its invitation to embrace it through committed action.

KEYWORDS

justice, struggle, action

BIOGRAPHY

Allan Aubrey Boesak (1946) is a South African theologian, liberation activist, and public intellectual whose life has been marked by a commitment to justice. Born in 1946 in Kakamas, Northern Cape, he was raised in a deeply religious household by his mother, Sarah Helene Boesak. She profoundly shaped his moral and theological

---

Hasselaar, Jan Jorrit, Mark van Vuuren, Julieta Matos Castaño, and Erik Borgman, eds. *Voices of Hope: Rediscovering and Building Hope for All.* Amsterdam: Amsterdam University Press / Central European University Press, 2026.

 DOI 10.5117/9789048577347-21

imagination, and Boesak has often credited her unshakable faith in the midst of poverty and apartheid violence as his earliest encounter with liberation theology. For him, this was not abstract theory but a lived conviction.

Boesak's education began at Gordon High School, a school designated for 'coloured' learners under apartheid. At the age of seventeen, he enrolled at the University of the Western Cape's theological seminary. He was ordained as a minister in the Dutch Reformed Mission Church in Paarl at the age of twenty-two. In Paarl, Boesak came face to face with people heavily affected by the apartheid policy of forced removals. He often mentions one congregant, Meraai Arendse, who had a profound impact on his life when she told him:

> You don't have to talk to me about Jesus [...]. I have known and loved him before you were born. What I want to know is this: What is God saying about this injustice? Why is God allowing this to happen?

This marked a turning point in his theology.

Allan Boesak later pursued postgraduate studies in the Netherlands at Kampen, where he encountered Reformed theology afresh, engaging thinkers like John Calvin (1509–1564), Abraham Kuyper (1837–1920), and Dietrich Bonhoeffer (1906–1945). A visit to the United States, where he met people like James Cone (1938–2018), further shaped his theological identity and deepened his critique of the apartheid church. As Tinyiko Samuel Maluleke mentions in Alan Boesak's biography: 'There, Boesak met the Black Messiah and bid farewell to the Jesus of Constantinian Christianity, without thorns but with a crown of laurels.' Boesak returned to South Africa during the height of political unrest following the Soweto Uprising of 1976. His charismatic public presence and prophetic rhetoric soon propelled him to national and international prominence as a leader in the Belhar confession process, as president of the World Alliance of Reformed Churches, and as founding member of the United Democratic Front.

Throughout his career, Boesak insisted that Christian faith cannot be separated from the struggle for justice. Whether from the pulpit, the podium, or the protest line, he has consistently challenged theologies that justify oppression, offering instead a vision of God as the defender of the poor, the stranger, and the oppressed. Though controversies have marked his later public life, Boesak remains a towering figure in South African theology and politics. For many in the Uniting Reformed Church in Southern Africa, he continues to be remembered as a prophetic voice – one who refused to separate spiritual integrity from political resistance. Tinyiko Maluleke's summary of Boesak is worth noting: 'He is a wordsmith and an orator, a preacher and debater, a scholar and a researcher, a man, a husband, and a father. Above all, he is human, all too human.'

ALLAN BOESAK ON HOPE

Although hope runs through all Boesak's writings, it is in his 2014 book *Dare We Speak of Hope? Searching for a Language of Life in Faith and Politics* that he confronts it most directly. The title is suggestive. Hope becomes for him 'a new language' that can speak as much about 'woundability' as about 'the righteousness of our strength', the latter phrase drawn from Steve Biko. Hope is not the 'opiate of the poor', he stresses, not a kind of 'triumphalist sermonising that bubbles over with joyous certitude'. Instead, Boesak links hope to what Dietrich Bonhoeffer calls 'a tremendous decision': the faithful witness – especially amid suffering – that we are not dreamers with our heads in the clouds, numbed by faith, but are instead 'faithful to the earth for the sake of things that are above'. For Boesak, these 'things that are above' are the very things that reflect God's will on earth: 'justice, peace, human worthiness, and the search for hope and a meaningful life'.

Boesak dares to speak about hope by exploring two striking images of God: God 'with the wounded knee' and God as 'a wailing woman'. The first draws on the theology of the Khoikhoi people, who call God 'Tsui//Goab'. the one who fought evil and came out limping. This, Boesak says, is the God of Scripture: not primarily 'a God of power and might' but one of 'woundedness and empathetic solidarity'. This God limps beside God's wounded children, standing between them and destruction. For Boesak, this is the ground of hope: not naïve optimism but 'our strength in the ongoing battles against that particular death called hopelessness'. Hope, then, is for the wounded. The second image goes further still. Drawing from the work of Old Testament theologian Juliana Claassens, Boesak insists that the liberator-God is not imperial or omnipotent but appears 'as a wailing woman, a mother, and midwife'. This God creates new life through grief, not dominion. It is not hope born from death but from defiant, life-giving acts.

Boesak warns that it is possible to speak of hope in a way that denies life. Hope becomes hollow when, in his words, it is 'bereaved of her children'. He turns to the African theologian St Augustine of Hippo, who once said that hope has two daughters, anger and courage – anger 'at the way things are' and courage 'to see that they do not remain the same'. These children are born amid suffering and despair. However, not all anger is hope-filled. Boesak makes clear that for him, true anger is not retributive or self-serving; it is 'righteous anger because of injustice done to others'. It is the refusal to accept the status quo when it degrades those made in God's image. It is anger at the arrogance of power, and it exposes false neutrality and stands with 'injured but unbowed dignity'. Likewise, courage is not dominance or control, according to Boesak; it is the resolve 'to stand up for the weak and exploited', the courage, as the Belhar Confession says, 'to stand where God stands, namely against injustice and with the wronged'.

For Boesak, it is important that 'hope and history rhyme'. He situates this vision historically by reflecting on Sol Plaatje, the first secretary-general of the African National Congress. In 1916, amid land dispossession, war, and betrayal, Plaatje wrote: 'The only thing that stands between us and despair is the thought that Heaven has not failed us.' Boesak does not see escapism here but rather fierce theological conviction that the struggle is God's, not ours alone. It is resisting the world's ideologies while being 'seduced by the dream of God', that is, the dream of justice, peace, and wholeness. Above all, he says, it is trusting that 'there is a God of justice ... who has taken sides ... and calls us to join the struggle'. Plaatje's 'Heaven' is not a distant realm but rather the presence of the God of the oppressed. It is the same God that Chief Albert Luthuli (1898–1967) alluded to years later when he was president-general of the African National Congress and amid equally terrifying circumstances: 'There is a witness to be borne, and God will not fail those who bear it fearlessly.' Although the Apartheid state declared its future as fixed, Luthuli clung to hope for dignity, peace, and freedom. Luthuli's refrain – 'the road to freedom is via the cross' – was no pious cliché. For him, says Boesak, the cross was the cost of resistance. It was about Jesus being condemned for his stand against oppressive powers. But it was also the source of hope: God comes alongside us and will not forsake those who suffer.

Boesak closes this reflection with an image of Christ who is unmistakeably located

> in the ghettos and squatter camps where poverty, hunger, and neglect reign supreme; in the silent and suffocating enclosures of domestic and sexual violence, where fear has dislodged love and mutual respect. [...] Where hopelessness claims the throne and despair proclaims supremacy.

There, he says, '[h]ope is waiting to be embraced, to be invited into the struggle for justice'. In the end, Boesak dares to write: 'To say "Jesus" is to say "justice", and to say "justice" is to say "hope"' ... which also implies that injustice is blasphemy.

REFERENCES AND BIBLIOGRAPHICAL INFORMATION

Boesak, A.A. (1976). *Farewell to Innocence: A Socio-Ethical Study of Black Theology and Black Power*. Ravan Press. (Published version of the author's doctoral dissertation)

Boesak, A.A. (2014). *Dare We Speak of Hope? Searching for a Language of Life in Faith and Politics*. Wm. B. Eerdmans Publishing Co.

Boesak, A.A. (2024). *The Fire, the River, and the Scorched Earth Between: Fifty Years of Black Liberation Theology through the Lens of Allan Aubrey Boesak* (Vols. 1–4).

Maluleke, T.S. (2017). 'The Making of Allan Aubrey Boesak: Theologian and Political Activist.' *Missionalia*, 45(1), 61–76.

Plaatjies van Huffel, M.A. (2018). 'The Unsettling Story about Allan Boesak's Involvement in the Struggle against Apartheid.' *Studia Historiae Ecclesiasticae*, 44(1), 1–23. https://doi.org/10.25159/2412-4265/3552

ABOUT THE AUTHOR

Marius Louw is minister at the English Reformed Church in Amsterdam and a PhD candidate at Stellenbosch University, South Africa and Vrije Universiteit Amsterdam, the Netherlands.

MARTHA NUSSBAUM

Hope against fear and passivity

BY MARK VAN VUUREN

ARTWORK BY JANWILLEM HOFTIJZER

ABSTRACT

This essay examines Martha Nussbaum's view that hope and fear share a common structure: both arise from caring about uncertain outcomes we cannot control. Since hope is vulnerable rather than self-protective, Nussbaum argues that we should choose it as a practical postulate, directing it toward good causes and cultivating it as a moral impulse.

KEYWORDS

vulnerability, choice, intention

BIOGRAPHY

Martha C. Nussbaum was born Martha Craven on 6 May 1947, in New York City. She is professor at the University of Chicago and one of the most well-known philosophers of our time. She holds 69 honorary doctorates and wrote numerous influential analyses on emotions, including love, grief, shame, compassion, and disgust.

Hasselaar, Jan Jorrit, Mark van Vuuren, Julieta Matos Castaño, and Erik Borgman, eds. *Voices of Hope: Rediscovering and Building Hope for All.* Amsterdam: Amsterdam University Press / Central European University Press, 2026.

 DOI 10.5117/9789048577347-22

Nussbaum studied theatre and classics at New York University, receiving a Bachelor's in 1969. She gradually moved to philosophy while at Harvard University, where she earned a Master's in 1972 and a doctorate in 1975. Her book *The Fragility of Goodness* from 1986, on ancient Greek ethics and Greek tragedy, established her name in the humanities. She taught at Harvard University until 1982, then at Brown University until 1995, and after that at the University of Chicago Law School. Nussbaum initiated her conversion to Judaism around 1986 and celebrated her *bat mitzvah* in 2008.

Combining her expertise in ethics, law, and economics, Nussbaum developed the so-called capability approach in collaboration with Nobel Prize laureate Amartya Sen. Many agree with the general idea that people should have the freedom to achieve the kind of lives they value. The capability approach explores both the means people need to live this fulfilling life, and the arrangements a society must make to improve access to these means. If a society is to count as minimally just, every citizen must have at least an acceptable amount of these capabilities. They include life and bodily integrity, the possibility to hold property and to participate in political and societal choices, and the ability to have emotions (i.e. not having one's emotional development blighted by fear and anxiety) and to play and be creative.

A dedicated political philosopher herself, in 2019 Nussbaum started a series of roundtables about controversial issues for students at the University of Chicago. It is meant as a way to address what Nussbaum considers the serious problem of political polarization among students.

MARTHA NUSSBAUM ON HOPE

Deeply disturbed by Donald Trump's first presidency, Nussbaum wrote a philosophical book called *The Monarchy of Fear* in 2019, which focuses on the topic of hope in the final chapter. What follows is a summary of that chapter in a few short quotes.

Nussbaum rejects the view that 'hope involves a desire for an outcome, combined with an assessment that this outcome is quite likely'. She believes that hope does not depend on our assessment of probabilities nor merely on a desire for something good; it must also concern something genuinely good and worth pursuing. In a way, hope and fear come from the same source: 'Both involve evaluation of an outcome as very important, both involve great uncertainty about the outcome, and both involve a good measure of passivity or lack of control.' Where fear is present, hope is present too, she states. However, there is a major difference. Hope is vulnerable, while fear is self-protective. In other words, 'Hope swells outward, fear shrinks back.'

Martha Nussbaum makes a distinction between idle hope and practical hope. In her view, 'hope involves a vision of the good world that might ensue, and, often at least, actions related to getting there.' However, she signals, sometimes 'hoping is inert and impotent, and may even distract from useful work'. This is idle hope, which only 'indulges in emotion and fantasy without work'. We should therefore be careful what images we focus on and what thoughts we summon up in our mental space. She is aligned with German philosopher Immanuel Kant (1724–1804), who believed that we have a duty during our lives to engage in actions that produce valuable social goals. Embracing hope thus means motivating ourselves to pursue those goals. Agreeing with Kant, she writes: 'we should choose hope as a "practical postulate", an attitude that we take on without sufficient reasons, for the sake of the good action it may enable'.

Hope is not good per se, Nussbaum contends. 'Hope itself is neutral: criminals have hope, dictators, tax evaders, fanatics of all sorts have hope. Indeed, we wish these people didn't have so much high hope, since they might then be less energetic in pursuing their bad goals. A languid, timorous Hitler would probably have done little damage to the world, whereas the hopeful visionary Hitler did untold damage.' In order to be good, hope needs good people committed to genuinely good causes. Ultimately, hope is meaningless without love. Without love for others, Nussbaum states, a life of detachment or even despair will make more sense than a life of hope, with its many demands. 'Stoicism and cynicism are perennial threats for the hopeful,' she writes. 'The cynic scoffs at the romantic dreams of hopers. The Stoic is less openly hostile but shrinks back from the waters of life into an insular detachment. Stoics promise us inner peace, proud independence, and a lofty superiority to fortune. Cynics say the world just isn't worth that much anyway. The life of detachment is "easier and safer".' Such people, Nussbaum quotes Cicero, 'are guilty of what might be called "passive injustice"'.

Nussbaum mentions five 'schools of hope' – spheres of life where hope can be cultivated. First and foremost, we have the sphere of the *arts*. Empathy is learned through reading, while dancing and singing are ways to 'share breath and bodily contact with one another'. This all helps to overcome fear. The second sphere is *Socratic reasoning*, which Nussbaum calls 'a practice of hope because it creates a world of listening, of quiet voices, and of mutual respect for reason'. Another sphere is *religion*, as it 'sustain[s] people in many ways in the crises of life and often serve as sources of hope – not just hope of salvation, if the religion talks of salvation, but also hope for and in our lives with one another on this earth'. *Protest movements* can also be seen as a school of hope. Nussbaum argues that we 'need this-worldly movements that give [us] a sense of solidarity in a good cause'. And finally, *accounts of justice* also help to cultivate hope, as people who hope for the future of their country need to have a vision of the goal for which they are striving. Here, her own capability approach is a case in point.

Thus, with a few broad strokes, Nussbaum depicts hope as a good impulse that should be cherished and cultivated, for the inevitable impulse of fear easily lures us into self-protective passivity. Hope is practical, focused on goodness and fuelled by faith.

REFERENCES AND BIBLIOGRAPHICAL INFORMATION

Nussbaum, M.C. (1986). *The Fragility of Goodness: Luck and Ethics in Greek Tragedy and Philosophy*. Cambridge University Press.

Nussbaum, M.C., & Sen, A. (Eds.). (1993). *The Quality of Life*. Clarendon Press.

Nussbaum, M.C. (2003). *Upheavals of Thought: The Intelligence of Emotions*. Cambridge University Press.

Nussbaum, M.C. (2019). *The Monarchy of Fear: A Philosopher Looks at our Political Crisis*. Simon & Schuster.

ABOUT THE AUTHOR

Mark van Vuuren is associate professor of positive organizing at the University of Twente, the Netherlands.

JONATHAN SACKS

A life in service of hope

BY JAN JORRIT HASSELAAR AND MIRIAM FELDMANN-KAYE

ARTWORK BY JANWILLEM HOFTIJZER

ABSTRACT

This essay explores Jonathan Sacks's view of hope as journey of small and courageous steps. Human beings are called to freedom by confronting and integrating conflicting interests within and between us. For Sacks, hope must be renewed in every context and generation, inviting people to take responsibility for a shared future.

KEYWORDS

courage, responsibility, renewal

BIOGRAPHY

Jonathan (Hebrew: Yaakov Zvi) Sacks (1948–2020) was born on 8 March 1948 into a traditional Orthodox Jewish family in the East End of London, the point of arrival for many Jewish immigrants. As a teenager, Jonathan Sacks attended Christ's College School in Finchley. Although this was a Christian school, many of the students were Jewish, and Sacks organized and led assemblies for them. The experience of making space for other convictions stim-

Hasselaar, Jan Jorrit, Mark van Vuuren, Julieta Matos Castaño, and Erik Borgman, eds. *Voices of Hope: Rediscovering and Building Hope for All.* Amsterdam: Amsterdam University Press / Central European University Press, 2026.
 DOI 10.5117/9789048577347-23

ulated his understanding that difference does not have to mean division, a point he articulated forcefully in his 2002 bestseller *The Dignity of Difference*.

In the summer of 1968, the young Jonathan Sacks was intellectually wrestling with the relation between Judaism and the modern world while studying philosophy at the University of Cambridge (called 'moral sciences' at the time). He set off with a scholarship to the United States and Canada and travelled via Greyhound public transport to meet several Jewish figures and leaders who went on to influence his thought, decisions, and entire oeuvre. Two encounters were particularly transformative. One of them was with Joseph B. Soloveitchik (1903–1993), a leading voice in North American Modern Orthodoxy, and the other one was Menachem Mendel Schneersohn (1902–1994), also known as the Lubavitcher Rebbe, leader of the Hassidic Chabad-Lubavitch movement.

What struck Sacks about them both was the depth of their commitment to the Jewish faith and life even as they engaged fully with the modern world. Rabbi Soloveitchik was open to the intellectual challenges of modern thought, notably that of Rudolph Otto and Søren Kierkegaard. The Lubavitcher Rebbe advanced his conviction that Jews have a responsibility toward the world as a whole, an approach largely emblematic of the Chabad-Lubavitch global movement. These two life-changing encounters in North America allowed Sacks to navigate the complex path between religious study and leadership (the rabbinate) and academic life. They prompted him to move beyond academia and towards positions of communal responsibility and Jewish religious leadership. Both Soloveitchik and the Lubavitcher Rebbe challenged Sacks to delve deeply into his Jewish and religious studies while fully engaging with the world around him. The Lubavitcher Rebbe asked him what he was doing for Jewish students in Cambridge, which led Sacks to take on a greater student leadership role in Cambridge. Ultimately, Sacks not only deepened his engagement with his community and society but also took up rabbinical studies to investigate Judaism's uniqueness not least in relation to the world.

In 1973, Sacks began Jewish Studies at Jews' College, the world's oldest rabbinical seminary and now called the London School of Jewish Studies. In 1978 he was appointed Rabbi of the Golders Green Synagogue, and in 1983 Rabbi of the Marble Arch Synagogue in London. He later became Principal of Jews' College, and in 1991 he was appointed Chief Rabbi of the United Hebrew Congregations of the Commonwealth. He was not only an influential voice within and for British Jewry but also an important public intellectual with impact far beyond Judaism, writing in *The Times* and presenting broadcasts for the BBC.

Sacks retired from his chief rabbinate in 2013 with a pamphlet entitled *A Judaism Engaged with the World*. Remaining active in writing and speaking, Jonathan Sacks passed away on 7 November 2020.

JONATHAN SACKS ON HOPE

Two important concepts Sacks developed while pursuing Jewish Studies are those of hope and optimism. He elaborated this initial framework by distinguishing sharply between the two, posing the question: what is the difference between optimism and hope? In *The Dignity of Difference* he argues:

> Optimism is the belief that things will get better. Hope is the faith that, together, we can make things better. Optimism is a passive virtue, hope is an active one. It takes no courage to be an optimist, but it takes a great deal of courage to have hope.

Sacks' understanding of hope is arguably derived from the narrative of the Exodus in the Bible. Many readers may think that the story of the Exodus is about the divine intervention of the ten plagues that liberated the Israelites from slavery in Egypt, but for Sacks, such a reading misses the full meaning of the narrative. He argues that to fully understand the Exodus, we must go beneath the surface of the biblical text itself. There is a second layer that tells another story. In his 2010 book *Covenant & Conversation: Exodus*, Sacks argues that the book of Exodus contains a number of double narratives. Their significance becomes clear when we put them together. As he points out:

- here are two battles: one immediately before, the other immediately after the crossing of the Reed Sea, the first against Pharaoh and his chariots, the second against the Amalekites
- there are two sets of stone tablets recording God's revelation at Mount Sinai, one before the episode of the Golden Calf, broken by Moses on his descent from the mountain, the second after the people have been forgiven for the Golden Calf
- God is revealed twice in a cloud of glory: once at Mount Sinai, the other time at the end of the book of Exodus, in the Tabernacle
- the Sinai covenant was declared twice: once by God, the second time by Moses while reading from 'the book of the covenant' he had written to record God's words
- there are two accounts of the construction of the Tabernacle: one before and the other after the Golden Calf

As Sacks sees it, in all these cases it is the same shift of responsibility that takes place: a movement from divine initiative to human endeavour. The Exodus thus tells a double story. The first of the paired episodes talks about an act done by God alone, while the second involves human participation.

According to Sacks, the transition from divine initiative towards human responsibility is the underlying theme of the book of Exodus. Humans are called to freedom by internalizing conflicting forms of interest. God wants humans to fight their own battles as beings created in his image. Sacks uses several phrases to describe this shift, one of which is 'politics of hope'. In Sacks's understanding, hope requires more than simply replicating the truths or patterns of life of previous generations. Hope must be born anew in every generation for each new context and period.

Especially during the second half of his chief rabbinate, Sacks explored the politics of hope in relation to societal issues. One can refer here to his book *The Dignity of Difference*, which tries to make space in society for ethnic and religious differences. Another example is his 2007 book *The Home We Build Together*, in which Sacks offers a new paradigm for British citizenship he calls 'integrated diversity'. In his 2015 book *Not in God's Name*, Sacks explores the root of violence and how Judaism, Christianity, and Islam are related to it. His ultimate plea is for these religions to become part of the solution for the problem of violence by living together as sisters and brothers.

REFERENCES AND BIBLIOGRAPHICAL INFORMATION

Sacks, J. (2002). *The Dignity of Difference: How to Avoid the Clash of Civilizations*. Continuum. (Rev. ed. published in 2011)

Sacks, J. (2010). *Covenant & Conversation: Exodus—The Book of Redemption*. Maggid Books.

Sacks, J. (2013). *A Judaism Engaged with the World*. www.rabbisacks.org/a-judaism-engaged-with-the-world/

Rabbi Sacks Legacy Trust: https://rabbisacks.org/

Public Engagement Through Digital Learning: The Philosophy of Rabbi Jonathan Sacks. Massive Online Open Course available at https://sites.biu.ac.il/en/jonathan-sacks-institute/MOOC

ABOUT THE AUTHORS

Jan Jorrit Hasselaar, economist and theologian, is associate professor of public theology and director of the Amsterdam Centre for Religion & Sustainable Development at Vrije Universiteit Amsterdam, the Netherlands. He is a research fellow at the University of the Free State, South Africa. Jan Jorrit is co-chair of the Global Network for Public Theology.

Miriam Feldmann-Kaye is assistant professor in the Department of Jewish Philosophy at Bar Ilan University, Israel.

RUSSEL BOTMAN

Hope as embodied public practice

BY DEMAINE SOLOMONS

ARTWORK BY JANWILLEM HOFTIJZER

ABSTRACT

This essay explores Russel Botman's understanding of hope as a discipline shaped by patient, repeated decisions. Hope remains within imperfect institutions long enough to press them toward justice. It rejects both despair and triumphalism, remaining modest, self-critical, and committed to transforming society through steady engagement.

KEYWORDS

discipline, justice, engagement

BIOGRAPHY

Professor Hayman Russel Botman (1953–2014) was born in Bloemfontein on 18 October 1953. After matriculating from Kliptown Senior Secondary School in Johannesburg, he entered the University of the Western Cape (UWC) to study theology. Already as an undergraduate, he showed a clear instinct for public engagement. He served on the Student Representative Council as public relations officer and helped to organize anti-apartheid protests on campus. The connection between intellectual formation and public responsibility appears early and never leaves his story.

Hasselaar, Jan Jorrit, Mark van Vuuren, Julieta Matos Castaño, and Erik Borgman, eds. *Voices of Hope: Rediscovering and Building Hope for All.* Amsterdam: Amsterdam University Press / Central European University Press, 2026.
 DOI 10.5117/9789048577347-24

His academic path at UWC was steady and distinguished. He earned a Bachelor of Arts in 1978, followed by a Bachelor of Theology in 1979, a Licentiate in Theology in 1981, a Master of Theology (cum laude) in 1984, and a Doctor of Theology in 1994. These qualifications sustained a vocation that moved comfortably between parish ministry, ecumenical work, and public theology. Ordained in 1982, Botman served as minister of the Wynberg congregation of the Dutch Reformed Church in Africa. During the next decade, he played an important role in the processes of church unification within the Reformed family of churches. This work culminated in the formation of the Uniting Reformed Church in Southern Africa, a decisive development in the South African ecclesial landscape and an early sign of his commitment to unity, reconciliation, and justice as inseparable concerns.

In 1994, he made a formal transition into academia when he accepted a senior lectureship in practical theology at UWC, where his leadership was quickly recognized. By 1999, he had been appointed associate professor and dean of the Faculty of Religion and Theology. When theology at UWC was later scaled down, Botman accepted an invitation from Stellenbosch University (SU) in 2000 to become professor of missiology, ecumenism, and public theology, a move that opened the next chapter of his institutional influence. His trajectory at SU was equally significant. In 2002, he was appointed vice rector for teaching, and five years later, he made history as the first person of colour to become rector and vice chancellor of the university. During this same period, he also served as president of the South African Council of Churches, underscoring his influence both in the church and in academia. Throughout these roles, questions of justice, transformation, and public responsibility remained central to his work.

As rector, Botman placed institutional renewal at the centre of his leadership. He worked to reposition Stellenbosch University as a multicultural university that could no longer remain untouched by the pain and complexity of South African society. The 2010 HOPE

Project expressed this commitment by seeking to align the university's research, teaching, and community engagement with concrete societal needs such as poverty, public health, democracy, sustainability, and social cohesion. Under his leadership, the university adopted Vision 2030, which identified broadening the knowledge base, promoting student success, deepening diversity, and strengthening systemic sustainability as strategic priorities.

Botman's work was cut short when he passed away unexpectedly in his sleep on 28 June 2014. His influence, however, continues to shape debates in South Africa about transformation, public theology, and the purpose of the university.

RUSSEL BOTMAN ON HOPE

Hope is often treated as a mood, something that rises briefly and then recedes, but in Botman's life and work, it takes on a far more demanding shape. Hope becomes a discipline formed through repeated decisions and through the patient work of remaining inside imperfect institutions long enough to press them toward justice.

To write about hope through Botman is therefore not to collect uplifting language but to trace how a South African theologian and university leader held together faith, justice, and public responsibility in a society still marked by the unfinished work of decolonization. The roots of this hope lie in the struggle against apartheid and the ecumenical movements that accompanied it, where Botman was shaped by the Belhar Confession (1982/1986) and its insistence that unity, reconciliation, and justice are marks of the church itself. In that setting, he observed that theological language can bless unjust orders or expose them, and that the word hope can either pacify or mobilize people.

For Botman, hope is closely linked to protest. It is a refusal to accept the finality of injustice or the inevitability of inherited hierarchies. For this reason, his hope is consistently this-worldly. Hope belongs precisely in the penultimate, in the fragile space in which human beings act, fail, repent, and try again.

All of this rests on a theological conviction. God's future does not license withdrawal from the present. Rather, it summons deeper responsibility in the present. Botman reads Christian hope as the expression of God's commitment to the world, not God's abandonment of it. The resurrection of Christ is therefore the assurance that history remains open, that injustice does not have the last word, and that human action still matters.

His hope rejects both despair and triumphalism, holding together a sober assessment of reality and moral resolve. It remains modest and self-critical because it is acutely aware of human limits and institutional failure. Hope is therefore never neutral for Botman. It leans toward those who live with the consequences of racialized inequality, poverty, and exclusion.

These lines of thought converged in his leadership at SU. His appointment as rector in 2007 placed him at the centre of an institution long associated with the intellectual formation of apartheid. While the symbolism of a black rector was obvious, he refused to confuse symbolism with transformation. The question for him was how hope could take institutional form. The HOPE Project was his response. It sought to align the university's core functions with the needs of society, making hope a criterion for academic work. The measure of a project is not only its disciplinary excellence but also its contribution to a more just and humane social order.

Three commitments stand out as defining features of Botman's engagement with hope and transformation. First, hope determines who is welcomed and who is enabled to thrive. Widening access for disadvantaged students and supporting their success were non-negotiable for Botman. Hope becomes visible in admissions, funding, student residence cultures, language policies, and in a willingness to unsettle inherited privilege. Second, Botman resisted the false choice between excellence and justice. Knowledge is never neutral; it either disrupts injustice or reinforces it. Hope therefore requires a redefined excellence, one in which social realities shape research priorities, teaching practices, and the kind of graduates the institution forms. Third, he understood transformation as ongoing and contested. Institutions move forward and stall. Symbols change while older habits persist. Hope, therefore, requires continuous self-critique. It listens to those at the margins who point out what remains unmoved, treating their testimony as the measure of transformation's truth rather than its rhetoric.

Botman's reflections on hope also reached beyond the campus. He resisted the reduction of the university to a private service provider. Higher education, in his view, carries responsibilities toward the broader society that funds it. A hopeful university asks what kind of professionals and leaders it forms and how they are likely to act in contexts marked by inequality, violence, ecological strain, and corruption. Here, his theological convictions again come into view. Human dignity does not rest on achievement but on being recognized by God. Exclusion from quality education is therefore not only a political issue but a theological concern. Hope becomes a way of naming the expectation that institutions align themselves with this given dignity rather than reinforce inherited social hierarchies.

Sadly, Botman's death left many of his projects unfinished. Yet his vision continues to surface in public debates, especially in the ways students and colleagues remember him. Several implications follow. First, hope can be intellectually rigorous. It begins with an unsparing reading of history, structures, and institutional cultures, identifying small but real spaces for responsible action. Second, his example resists passivity. On his account, hope is incompatible with spectatorship. Theology, church life, and higher education must face the question of what they do with the hope they proclaim. Hope demands decisions about budgets, appointments, partnerships, curricula, and public speech. Third, hope remains close to those who live with the consequences of injustice. A hopeful institution listens attentively to communities that still experience exclusion, allowing their perspectives to expose where transformation is stalling.

Botman's life poses a direct question: how will those who remember him carry forward the work he outlined? The answer will differ across contexts. To speak of hope in his terms is already to have taken a position. It is to affirm that history remains open under God's future, that institutions can and should change, and that those who have benefited most from unjust orders carry a particular responsibility. In this sense, Russel Botman offers more than an inspiring personal story. He provides a concrete, intellectually rigorous, and theologically grounded account of hope that insists that the work toward a more just future remains possible, necessary, and unfinished.

REFERENCES AND BIBLIOGRAPHICAL INFORMATION

Anthony, E. (2020, October 28). 'Rector's Pedagogy of Hope Lauded.' *Netwerk24*.

Botman, H.R. (2007). *A Multicultural University with a Pedagogy of Hope for Africa* [Installation address as Rector and Vice-Chancellor]. Stellenbosch University.

Botman, H.R. (2011). *The Case for the Relevant University*. Stellenbosch University.

Smit, D.J. (2015). '"Making History for the Coming Generation": On the Theological Logic of Russel Botman's Commitment to Transformation.' *Stellenbosch Theological Journal*, 1(2), 607–632.

van Rinsum, H. (2014). 'Critical Hope: Deconstructing the Politics of Hope at a South African University.' In V. Bozalek, B. Leibowitz, R. Carolissen, & M. Boler (Eds.), *Discerning Critical Hope in Educational Practices* (pp. 82–91). Routledge.

Waghid, Y. (2011). 'Education and Hope: Stellenbosch University in the Twenty-First Century: Initiating Debate.' *South African Journal of Higher Education*, 25(1), 5–13.

ABOUT THE AUTHOR

Demaine Solomons is associate professor of systematic theology and ethics at Stellenbosch University, South Africa.

POPE LEO XIV

United in the oneness of Christ

BY ERIK BORGMAN

ARTWORK BY JANWILLEM HOFTIJZER

ABSTRACT

This essay reflects on Pope Leo XIV's understanding of hope, inspired by people whose everyday actions uplift others and serve as living expressions of hope. He situates hope within a world undergoing profound transformations, urging that love for one another serve as the unifying force that carries communities through such change.

KEYWORDS

unity, renewal, love

BIOGRAPHY

Robert Francis Prevost (1955) was elected pope on 8 May 2025, in the middle of the Jubilee that his predecessor, Pope Francis, had dedicated to hope. 'Pilgrims of Hope' was the motto of the Jubilee and 'Hope will not disappoint' the title of the document announcing it. At the moment of his election, Prevost – a canon lawyer born in Chicago – was serving as prefect of the Dicastery for Bishops, the Vatican office

Hasselaar, Jan Jorrit, Mark van Vuuren, Julieta Matos Castaño, and Erik Borgman, eds. *Voices of Hope: Rediscovering and Building Hope for All.* Amsterdam: Amsterdam University Press / Central European University Press, 2026.

 DOI 10.5117/9789048577347-25

responsible for all matters concerning the exercise of the episcopal ministry in the Roman Catholic Church. Previously, from 2002 to 2013, he had been Prior General, the worldwide head of the Order of Saint Augustine, of which he has been a member since 1977. From 2015 to 2023, he served as bishop of Chiclayo, Peru.

Regarding his time as a bishop in Peru, Pope Leo declared that he was happy to have experienced 'a Church that accompanies people in their sorrows, in their joys, in their struggles and in their hopes'. This he considers to be 'an antidote to the spreading structural indifference that does not take seriously the drama of people who are stripped, robbed, sacked and reduced to poverty'. A commitment to the betterment of their living conditions in their own movements is, in the pope's view, a force against what he calls a 'globalization of powerlessness'.

This conviction seems to be rooted in his own life as an Augustinian friar. Speaking to women and men living the consecrated lives of monks and friars, nuns and sisters, Pope Leo XIV challenged them to be witnesses to 'the eschatological dimension of Christian life'. Fully engaged in the world, they should at the same time strive towards eternity beyond this world. The task of the religious is to seek to live in fullness through prayer to God. God is 'the eternal horizon that transcends the realities of this world'. The religious should seek to orient these worldly realities 'toward that Sunday without sunset': the ultimate destination of everything. This mission should be fulfilled in their concrete way of life. By being 'truly poor, meek, eager for holiness, merciful and pure of heart', women and men living the religious life can be among those who bring to the world the peace of God that is rooted in hope.

POPE LEO XIV ON HOPE

Much as Pope Francis did, Pope Leo XIV stresses what the Roman Catholic Church has since the 1980s called 'the preferential option for the poor'. In the exhortation *Dilexi te*, which was begun by his predecessor and completed and promulgated by Pope Leo in October 2025, the following is stated, in a spirit that reflects both Francis and Leo:

> [T]he Lord's words of hope and liberation are addressed first of all to [the poor]. ... And the Church, if she wants to be Christ's Church, must be a Church of the Beatitudes, one that makes room for the little ones and walks with the poor, a place where the poor have a privileged place.

Here Leo expressly put forward the example of religious sisters who were wholly dedicated to a mission of elevating the poor.

Their pedagogy was simple: closeness, patience, and gentleness. They taught by the example of their lives before teaching with words. In times of widespread illiteracy and systemic exclusion, these consecrated women were beacons of hope. Their mission was to form hearts, teach people to think, and promote dignity. By combining a life of piety and dedication to others, they fought abandonment with the tenderness of those who educate in the name of Christ.

In other words, they embodied – and still embody – hope.

Thus, during the first half year of his pontificate, Pope Leo XIV was first and foremost the inheritor of Pope Francis' theology of hope. In this line, he insisted that hope is found in the preferential option for those whose only hope is in God, as the path toward a future worthy of human beings. Nonetheless, Pope Leo has also added a few accents of his own.

First, there is his chosen name – Leo – which spiritually links his pontificate to that of Leo XIII, the originator of what came to be called Catholic Social Teaching whose papacy lasted from 1878 to 1903. This was a time of profound change in the social fabric of society caused by the industrial revolution that led to deep ideological tensions, in society in general but also within the Catholic Church. Today, Leo XIV is convinced we live in a new kind of industrial revolution driven by artificial intelligence. In line with his namesake, the new pope stressed that during this change of epochs we should be united by our love for one another. The church is called, first and foremost, to bear witness to this love, which at the very least means – as Leo XIII put it in 1891 in his encyclical *Rerum Novarum* – that 'to exercise pressure upon the indigent and the destitute for the sake of gain, and to gather one's profit out of the need of another, is condemned by all laws, human and divine'. Keeping these laws ingrained in our human existence should be enough to combat 'strife and all its causes' effectively.

Second, the influence of Saint Augustine is palpable. Being his spiritual son is important to Pope Leo. As Prior General of the Augustinian Order, he underscored, in line with Augustine, that authority is above all a service. A leader must first listen to what the Spirit is saying in the people so that projects of the Spirit can be carried out freely and willingly. A Prior is then called to help discern and implement what the Spirit inspires the community to do. This is the understanding of leadership that Pope Leo brings into his papacy. The motto that is part of his Coat of Arms is also taken from Saint Augustine: *In Illo uno unum* ('In the One, we are one'). This means that, as Augustine himself explains, 'although we Christians are many, in the one Christ we are one' and united. To find this unity again in a polarized church and to express it effectively is for Pope Leo of the utmost importance. It would make the Church a beacon of hope in a dangerously divided world.

To re-learn and express this unity, not only within the Roman Catholic Church but also in the church's active relation to the world, the faithful should practice concrete acts of charity. According to *Dilexi te*: 'Remaining in the realm of ideas and theories, while failing to give them expression through frequent and practical acts of charity, will eventually cause even our most cherished hopes and aspirations to weaken and fade away.' Although he fully endorses the idea of 'structural sin' and the need for structural solutions to poverty, oppression, and exclusion, Leo XIV stresses the importance of what he calls 'almsgiving', that is, free and concrete acts of charity in response to concrete situations of need. As written in *Dilexi te*, 'almsgiving will touch and soften our hardened hearts'. If carried out with tact, intelligence, diligence, and responsibility, it enables those in distress to experience not abandonment but the affirmation of being seen and taken seriously in their situation. It teaches those who give alms to reach out and touch the suffering flesh of the poor in order to foster true solidarity. That solidarity is an expression of the love of God and the foundation of hope.

REFERENCES AND BIBLIOGRAPHICAL INFORMATION

Leo XIV (2025, May 18). *Homily during the Eucharistic Celebration for the Beginning of the Pontificate*. Vatican. https://www.vatican.va/content/leo-xiv/en/homilies/2025/documents/20250518-inizio-pontificato.html

Leo XIV (2025, October 4). *Dilexi te: On Love for the Poor* [Apostolic exhortation]. Vatican. https://www.vatican.va/content/leo-xiv/en/apost_exhortations/documents/20251004-dilexi-te.html

Leo XIV (2025, October 9). *Homily during the Eucharistic Celebration for the Jubilee of the Consecrated Life*. Vatican. https://www.vatican.va/content/leo-xiv/en/homilies/2025/documents/20251009-giubileo-vita-consacrata.html

Leo XIV (2025, October 23). *Address to the Participants in the World Meeting of Popular Movements*. Vatican. https://www.vatican.va/content/leo-xiv/en/speeches/2025/october/documents/20251023-movimenti-popolari.html

ABOUT THE AUTHOR

Erik Borgman is a lay Dominican and professor emeritus of public theology at Tilburg University, the Netherlands.

THABO MAKGOBA

Hope as a liberation process

BY JAN JORRIT HASSELAAR

ARTWORK BY JANWILLEM HOFTIJZER

ABSTRACT

This essay explores Thabo Makgoba's view of hope as an ongoing liberation process revealed in small, humane actions that shift conditions toward dignity and justice. These acts can grow expansively, like 'small steps becoming islands of hope and together forming landscapes of hope'.

KEYWORDS

Ubuntu, Indaba, liberation

BIOGRAPHY

Thabo Makgoba is Archbishop of Cape Town and Metropolitan of the Anglican Church of Southern Africa. In 2007, he became the youngest person to be elected to this office. Makgoba is the immediate successor to Archbishop Desmond Tutu (1986–1996) and Archbishop Njongonkulu Ndungane (1996–2007).

Hasselaar, Jan Jorrit, Mark van Vuuren, Julieta Matos Castaño, and Erik Borgman, eds. *Voices of Hope: Rediscovering and Building Hope for All.* Amsterdam: Amsterdam University Press / Central European University Press, 2026.
 DOI 10.5117/9789048577347-26

Thabo Cecil Makgoba was born on 15 December 1960 in Tlhabine, Limpopo, near Makgoba's Kloof. Makgoba's Kloof is named after his Makgoba clan. In his autobiography *Faith and Courage: Praying with Mandela* (2019), Makgoba describes the beauty of Makgoba's Kloof with its mountains, valleys, rivers, and mists. The connection of the Makgobas with this land and environment is also expressed in the clan's praise poem:

> Ke Makgoba a sefara (Makgoba of the shoot)
> A Sefara sa molapong (The shoot of the valley)
> Ke Tlou (Elephant)
> Tloukgolo ditswa Bolepye (Great elephants from Bolepye)
> Bolopye Ba tlhaku di a liwa (Bolepye where there is abundance)
> A gee Tlou! (Hail Elephants!)

Makgoba's Kloof is not only a land of great joy but also one of great pain. The pain began when the Boer republicans began to take control over Makgoba's Kloof in 1881 and initiated the expansion of white settlements. Kgoši (King) Mamphoku Makgoba, the great-grandfather of Thabo Makgoba, resisted the demarcation of his land for settler use and the paying of taxes. The war against Kgoši Makgoba was finally triggered when the government started applying forced removals in the 1890s. After fighting bravely, Kgoši Makgoba was eventually beheaded in 1895 and the Makgoba clan was displaced by force to a government farm in Makapanstad near Pretoria.

Thabo Makgoba grew up in Alexandra township, Johannesburg during what some would describe as the era of 'high apartheid', after his father had moved there as a migrant worker. In 1974, the family was forced under apartheid laws to move from Alexandra to Pimville, Soweto. Makgoba received a Diploma in theology from St. Paul's College in Grahamstown. He also obtained a Master's in educational psychology from the University of the Witwatersrand and a PhD from the University of Cape Town. Makgoba served as Bishop of Queenstown, then as Bishop of Grahamstown. He is chair of the international development and humanitarian agency Christian Aid.

Makgoba has served as Chancellor of the University of the Western Cape and is a former chair of the Anglican Communion Environmental Network and of the Anglican Communion Science Commission. He served as President of the South African Council of Churches and as a Board Member of NGOs and ecumenical and interfaith bodies. He has participated in several World Economic Forum meetings in Davos and plays an active role in numerous international peacekeeping initiatives. Makgoba is married to Lungi Manona, and they have two children, Nyakallo and Paballo. He has received several honorary degrees and awards.

THABO MAKGOBA ON HOPE

On many occasions, Archbishop Makgoba has made the distinction between 'the old struggle' and 'the new struggle' in South Africa. In the opening lecture of the symposium 'Rediscover and Build Hope for All' (Rome, 2025), Makgoba stated:

> Our forebears in South Africa brought us out of the wilderness of colonialism and apartheid into the Promised Land of a non-racial democracy; it is now up to us to build that Promised Land. In order to do that, I have been advocating for the last decade what I call the New Struggle, a new struggle which replaces the old struggle against apartheid.

The old struggle is the struggle against apartheid. For South Africa to flourish, Makgoba is convinced that people need to embark on a new struggle: the struggle for an equal and inclusive South Africa. According to Makgoba, there are many daunting challenges that are part of the new struggle, for example poverty, (youth) unemployment, corruption, inequality, inadequate education, lack of adequate water supplies and good sanitation, domestic violence, and climate change. For Makgoba, underlying these challenges is a deeper challenge to repudiate the values that underpinned colonialism and apartheid: narrow self-interest; callous selfishness; and the pursuit of personal gain, power, status, and material wealth, regardless of the consequences for other people or the planet.

According to Makgoba, in the past two decades in South Africa, the culture has tended to organize itself around and reward the 'me'. In this consumer culture, 'we' isn't popular, and the values of Ubuntu are slipping away. What is more, since the global financial crisis of 2008, Makgoba has come to realize that the new struggle should not be limited to South Africa. Across the world, also in Europe and the United States, there are people who are left behind by the economic and political system.

In his address to the Provincial Synod of the Anglican Church of Southern Africa (2024), Makgoba asked whether, in the midst of all these challenges, we are fully aware of the nature and the power of the Holy Spirit in us which raised Christ from the dead. For inspiration, he draws on the wisdom of spiritual ancestors: 'to remind us of the power, the life force, which will enable us to overcome despair as we face the challenges which beset us, and to break down those ramparts which surround us. I speak, of course, of the power of hope.' Makgoba often refers to one of the great saints of Africa, Augustine of Hippo, who said that hope has two beautiful daughters, anger and courage – anger at the way things are, and courage to ensure that they do not stay that way. At the same time, Makgoba is very critical of the use of the word 'hope'. For him, hope is not a nebulous, pie-in-the-sky concept. Hope also does not lie primarily in historical events. This becomes clear, Makgoba argues, in how people in South Africa have often pinned their hopes on the liberation event of 1994 – the first democratic election and the coming to power of a liberation movement. 'However, the hope of 1994 has mostly dwindled in South Africa despite the promising new constitution, the dismantling of Apartheid, the end of traditional colonialism, and free elections and other rights enshrined by the rule of law.'

Makgoba draws inspiration from Professor Jacobus Vorster (North-West University), who argues that Jürgen Moltmann's groundbreaking work based on his 1964 book *Theology of Hope* can provide guidance in the quest for 'tangible hope' in South Africa. In an article in HTS *Teologiese Studies/Theological Studies* (2023), Vorster writes:

> Moltmann's thesis is that the biblical message of hope as founded in revelation, promise and historical eschatology under the reign of the living God is that hope does not lie primarily in historic events, but in the movements brought about by the spirit of the living God founded on the crucified and resurrected Christ. There were many events of liberation in the history of Israel such as the exodus and returns from exile. But hope rooted in historic events soon faded also in their case.

In line with Vorster, Makgoba considers hope not as an event but rather as an ongoing liberation process built on the often-small signs of what Moltmann describes as 'the living, moving God' working through small acts that are the witnesses of God's Kingdom. For Makgoba, such an understanding of hope is not simply about good deeds but about deeds infused with love, which in the public domain means deeds infused with justice.

Makgoba has actively contributed to hope in the public domain by pioneering the concept of *Indaba* in relation to contemporary challenges. *Indaba* is an indigenous African concept that describes purposeful gatherings to discern the needs of a community. Makgoba uses Makgoba's Kloof as a point of reference for this alternative to confrontational modes of ways of talking in which the other is often seen as wrong. His point of departure is that we are all gifted and should cooperate for the common good, to achieve something bigger than ourselves, that none of us can achieve alone.

Makgoba has applied the concept of *Indaba* to different situations, including tensions in the worldwide Anglican Communion and peacekeeping initiatives. The aim is to encourage courageous dialogue in a transparent, honest, and constructive manner, and to support decision-making and consensus-building. Since 2015, Makgoba has promoted *Indaba* in the mining industry in an initiative called *Courageous Conversations*. This initiative brings together mining communities, executives, labour leaders, government, and people of faith. *Courageous*

Conversations aims to create a space where all parties can meet, converse, build trust, and strengthen partnerships, thereby repositioning the sector as a partner in long-term sustainable development.

For Makgoba, hope has the potential to multiply. Therefore, he ended his opening remarks at the *Rediscover and Build Hope for All* symposium with these words: 'Small steps taken in hope can become islands of hope and as they come together we can in turn create landscapes of hope.'

REFERENCES AND BIBLIOGRAPHICAL INFORMATION

Makgoba, T. (2019). *Faith & Courage: Praying with Mandela* (Foreword by G. Machel). Society for Promoting Christian Knowledge.

Makgoba, T. (2024, October 23). *Hope and Forgiveness: Tutu Jonker Memorial Lecture, University of the Free State.* https://archbishop.anglicanchurchsa.org/2024/10/tutu-jonker-memorial-lecture-at.html

Makgoba, T. (2025, June 2). *Rediscovering and Building Hope for All.* https://archbishop.anglicanchurchsa.org/2025/06/rediscovering-and-building-hope-for-all.html

Nesbitt, P.D. (2017). *Indaba!: A Way of Listening, Engaging, and Understanding Across the Anglican Communion.* Church Publishing, Inc.

Vorster, J.M. (2023). 'Six Decades of Moltmann's Theology of Hope and Tangible Hope in South Africa Today.' *HTS Teologiese Studies / Theological Studies,* 79(1). https://doi.org/10.4102/hts.v79i1.8988

ABOUT THE AUTHOR

Jan Jorrit Hasselaar, economist and theologian, is associate professor of public theology and director of the Amsterdam Centre for Religion & Sustainable Development at Vrije Universiteit Amsterdam, the Netherlands. He is a research fellow at the University of the Free State, South Africa. Jan Jorrit is co-chair of the Global Network for Public Theology.

IMTIAZ SOOLIMAN

Hope in the face of disaster

BY GRANT WALTERS, ABIGAIL HOPLEY AND MCEBISI PINYANA

ARTWORK BY JANWILLEM HOFTIJZER

ABSTRACT

This essay explores Imtiaz Sooliman's view of hope as a necessity woven into everyday life. In moments of crisis, everything cries out for hope, and social action becomes its clearest expression. For Sooliman, hope becomes apparent when people respond with empathy and when communities offer warmth and support.

KEYWORDS

response, empathy, community

BIOGRAPHY

Imtiaz Sooliman was born in 1962 in Potchefstroom in northwestern South Africa. He started his schooling in Potchefstroom but moved to Sastri College in Durban in 1978. He qualified as a medical doctor at the University of Natal Medical School in 1984 but gave up his medical career to pursue the field of humanitarian aid. For him, humanitarian work transcends the boundaries of race, religion, culture, class, and geography.

Hasselaar, Jan Jorrit, Mark van Vuuren, Julieta Matos Castaño, and Erik Borgman, eds. *Voices of Hope: Rediscovering and Building Hope for All.* Amsterdam: Amsterdam University Press / Central European University Press, 2026.

 DOI 10.5117/9789048577347-27

As a student, and later as a medical doctor and active member of civil society, Sooliman has been involved in several associations, religious organizations, and school-governing bodies.

In 1992, he established the Gift of the Givers Foundation. The organization is impartial and apolitical and aims to serve with compassion, kindness, and mercy. The foundation has developed into one of the most respected international humanitarian agencies. In its first 13 years, it donated more than 160 million rand to 22 countries, including South Africa. It was the first nonprofit agency to be accredited by Proudly South African, and in 2003, Sooliman's organization became the first in South African history to receive 60 million rand from the South African Government for humanitarian aid in KwaZulu-Natal and the Eastern Cape. One of the notable gifts that he organized was the donation of a well-equipped field hospital first used during the Bosnian War. The Gift of the Givers Foundation is the largest non-governmental disaster response organization of African origin on the continent. It has now donated over 6 billion rand in aid (approx. 300 million euro).

The Gift of the Givers continues to concern itself with alleviating physical and emotional suffering. The foundation provides disaster relief, primary healthcare clinics, feeding schemes, water purification, and water wells. It distributes new blankets, clothing, and food parcels. It donates bursaries, gives educational support, and provides toys for the underprivileged. It supports agricultural self-help schemes, job creation, counselling services, and drug rehabilitation. It runs HIV and AIDS programmes, skills-development training, and life-altering workshops.

All of this depends heavily on the dedication, energy, and leadership of Imtiaz Sooliman. His foundation mobilized help for Haiti in the wake of the earthquake disaster. He has also played a significant role in most South African communities during the Covid-19 pandemic. His latest relief activities were to help in the fire disasters in the Western Cape and water challenges in the Eastern Cape. All the foundation's humanitarian work is carried out in collaboration with faith communities, civil society, and government.

IMTIAZ SOOLIMAN ON HOPE

In 1992, Imtiaz Sooliman received a message from his spiritual leader in Istanbul, Turkey, Sufi Sheikh Muhammed Saffer Effendi al Jerrahi Se:

> My son, you will form an organisation. The name will be *Waqful Waqifin*, and that name is translated into 'Gift of the Givers'. You will serve all people of all races, of all religions, of all colours, of all classes, of all political affiliations and of any geographical location. You will serve them unconditionally.

Imtiaz Sooliman immediately heeded the calling. He returned to South Africa and established the Gift of the Givers Foundation, leaving a flourishing career as a medical doctor behind him. This transition from doctor to humanitarian was in a way both seamless and simple. He was driven by the same basic principles that led to his becoming a medical doctor: respect, care, professionalism, and dedication. Ultimately, Sooliman's passion for humanitarianism is grounded in the solid belief in the common humanity that unites us all. His fervour for and belief in humankind is what really motivates and energizes him. The reason behind this is his faith.

Hope is a necessity, according to Imtiaz Sooliman, but in our efforts and actions often seem sorely lacking. Speaking on Human Rights Day (2021), he stated that any political party that creates discord in South Africa 'can never be trusted to serve in government in the best interest of the nation'. He pointed out how political parties garner the support of the electorate by making the promise that they are there to 'strive for a better life for all'. However, when ego, opportunism, self-aggrandizement, inflammatory language, and irrational behaviour take over the psyche of people and shape their formation, the actions that follow are intrinsically anti-patriotic, treacherous, immoral, devoid of spirituality, and akin to agent provocateurs aimed at destroying communities, relationships, trust, and the economy – the absolute opposite of what they proclaim to be striving for.

Each day in our lives we live through hope. At times weary and wounded, our hearts thirst for truth, goodness, and beauty, and we dream of light that no darkness can dispel. Everything within and outside of us cries out for hope and continues to seek, even without knowing it, the closeness of God. The Gift of the Givers serves as a vehicle that brings about light in the midst of darkness and hope in hopeless situations. The visibility of the Gift of Givers in places of disaster is in itself a sign of hope.

In the wake of uncertainty in South Africa (2022), as the country marks one year since the widespread and politically driven looting and destruction of economic hubs in KwaZulu-Natal and parts of Gauteng, a sombre mood has set in. With the massive increases in the price of fuel and the cost of living, the rolling blackouts delivered by the South African electricity giant Eskom, and many families left scrambling to survive, South Africans have found themselves in a despondent mood. The Gift of the Givers has been a saving grace for the country, with many turning to Sooliman and his team to save them from despair. While the organization continues to cater to the needs of anyone in difficult circumstances, Sooliman says more needs to be done to ensure fewer and fewer people find themselves in such a situation. This can be done through active citizenry, he says: 'The country doesn't belong to the government. The government was not elected to serve themselves, and so it is up to each citizen to not allow anyone or any organisation to take South Africa from us.'

In his view, spirituality, morality, values, and ethics need to be at the forefront of every citizen's life in their decisions and their actions. Listing these four key traits, Sooliman says every citizen needs to snap out of their sombre mood and start the work. Saving the country from collapse and realizing a brighter and prosperous South Africa cannot be done by one group alone. The success of South Africa depends on every citizen. 'You have to be more aware; you have to stand up. There is strength in civil society and every person must be armed with the support of their community to better the country,' he said. Looking back at the 9-18 July 2021 unrest that saw Gift of the Givers traversing the length and breadth of KwaZulu-Natal in order to offer food, aid, and support, Sooliman said the warm response from communities, the eagerness to help each other, and the empathy shown to those who lost so much was the defining moment for him: 'This is why I say there is hope.'

REFERENCES AND BIBLIOGRAPHICAL INFORMATION

Gift of the Givers Foundation. (n.d.). *Gift of the Givers*. https://giftofthegivers.org/.

Morton, S. (2021). *Imtiaz Sooliman and the Gift of the Givers: A Mercy to All*. Bookstorm. (Original work published in 2014).

ABOUT THE AUTHORS

Grant Bradley Walters is the bishop of the Diocese of Port Elizabeth in the Anglican Church of Southern Africa, South Africa.

Abigail Hopley is personal assistant and acting chaplain to Archbishop Thabo Makgoba and priest at Good Shepherd Protea, Kirstenbosch, in the Anglican Church of Southern Africa, South Africa.

Mcebisi Pinyana is the bishop of the Diocese of Grahamstown in the Anglican Church of Southern Africa, South Africa.

CHRISTIAN WIMAN

Hope as loyalty to one's deepest yearnings

BY MARK VAN VUUREN

ARTWORK BY JANWILLEM HOFTIJZER

ABSTRACT

This essay explores how Christian Wiman's work makes us experience hope as something fragile and felt. In his writing, hope hurts when absent and remains elusive even when near, being a liminal presence that flickers at the edge of experience. In Wiman's writings, we experience that hope never extinguishes, yet it is never something we can fully grasp.

KEYWORDS

fragility, yearning, persistence

BIOGRAPHY

Christian Wiman is an American poet and essayist and the Clement-Muehl Professor of Communication Arts at Yale Divinity School. He is known for his deeply reflective writings on faith, mortality, and the human condition. Born in 1966 in Texas, Wiman grew up in a rural,

Hasselaar, Jan Jorrit, Mark van Vuuren, Julieta Matos Castaño, and Erik Borgman, eds. *Voices of Hope: Rediscovering and Building Hope for All.* Amsterdam: Amsterdam University Press / Central European University Press, 2026.
 DOI 10.5117/9789048577347-28

religious environment that would later inform much of his spiritual and poetic explorations. He attended Washington and Lee University and later completed graduate work at Stanford University as a Wallace Stegner Fellow in poetry.

An important biographical element in his work is the diagnosis of a rare and life-threatening cancer in his late 30s. This catalyzed a profound spiritual reawakening, which he chronicled in his 2013 memoir *My Bright Abyss*. In both poetry and prose, Wiman's work bridges the sacred and the secular. Wiman writes at the intersection of his life as a Christian (continuously wrestling with God and the church) and as a cancer patient (having survived three sure deathbeds thanks to the just-in-time arrival of highly experimental treatments that cured him).

From 2003 to 2013, Wiman was editor of *Poetry* magazine, which made him the ultimate authority in the United States to decide what counts as poetry. His own poetry, marked by precision, musicality, and emotional depth, often grapples with suffering, doubt, and the search for God in a secular age. Wiman edited anthologies of poems built around single words, in order to explore 'what might that one word mean'. He collected poems about *Joy* (2017) and about *Home* (2021). These are brilliant collections, also for readers not too familiar with poetry. Most recently, in 2023, he published *Zero at the Bone*, a book about hope – or, more precisely, a book against despair.

Throughout it all, he haunts reality and truth, finding forms in language. Language is for him the 'cage in search of a bird,' as Franz Kafka put it.

CHRISTIAN WIMAN ON HOPE

Most of Wiman's later work deals with faith and hope, struggle and truth. Yet it is impossible to find a theory of hope in his work. Instead, he gives his readers something else: hope can be experienced in reading his work. For example, in his 50 *Entries Against Despair*, there is much despair to be found, and it is only between the lines that the reader senses how this litany is ultimately against despair. Thus it becomes clear that while hope may seem nice to have, it also hurts. One can physically feel the craving of something very important that is just not there. The yearning for some presence, some realization in the face of its ongoing absence, is heightened by the intensity of your chase to get there, to get it, to make it real. Wiman makes clear that hoping involves suffering – and that it is worth it. It can be soothing to have language for the expression of such cravings and yearnings.

Wiman is brutally honest in his search for what is real in life and almost blasphemous in his expression of faith. Why? Because he genuinely looks for a way, a way out. As poet Robert Frost wrote in *A Servant to Servants*:

> [Someone said:] the best way out is always through.
> and I agree to that, or in so far
> as that I can see no way out but through.

Wiman clings to whatever he finds. He cites Abraham Joshua Heschel (1907–1972), who wrote that 'faith is primarily faithfulness to a time when we had faith'. We remember these moments of intensity and closeness to God, Wiman notes, and 'we endeavour to remain true to them. It's a tenuous and tenacious discipline of memory and hope'. It would be disloyal to oneself to treat these experiences with contempt. Loyalty is also required for joy, home, love, and hope. The very existence of these ideas points towards their reality: '[I]f there is no such thing as a true home for us in this world, how is it that we have such a strong sense for what it is?', he wonders in the introduction to the anthology on *Home*. These experiences inevitably leave one with a sense of lacking, however. As Wiman said in a 2024 interview:

> Even joy is shadowed with sorrow in this life. C.S. Lewis in 'Surprised by Joy', says that it makes us feel homesick for a home we didn't realize we had, which I think is a great way of putting it. There's a poet I love, Richard Wilbur, and he looks at a brook, and at the end of the brook, he

> describes it perfectly all the way through, and at the end he says, 'Joy's trick is to supply / dry lips with what can cool and slake, / leaving them dumbstruck also with an ache / nothing can satisfy.' So that feeling of being absolutely fulfilled all of a sudden and yet also, not destitute, but there's a lack, there's some lack that you're aware of, which I think is God.

As said earlier, neither easy answers nor systematic conceptualizations of hope can be found in Wiman's work, but the reader can sometimes experience hope in his poetry. One example of this is the following poem, entitled 'From a Window'. Imagine a patient in a hospital room who is 'incurable', whose only available truth is 'the truth of grieving'. Outside, there is a tree with a swarm of birds sitting in its branches. And then, at once, the birds fly away. The tree is not just the tree. It is far more than that. And the truth is more than what catches the eye. It flies 'heavenwards'.

> Incurable and unbelieving
> in any truth but the truth of grieving,
>
> I saw a tree inside a tree
> rise kaleidoscopically
>
> as if the leaves had livelier ghosts.
> I pressed my face as close
>
> to the pane as I could get
> to watch that fitful, fluent spirit
>
> that seemed a single being undefined
> or countless beings of one mind
>
> haul its strange cohesion
> beyond the limits of my vision
>
> over the house heavenwards.
> Of course I knew those leaves were birds.

Of course that old tree stood
exactly as it had and would

(but why should it seem fuller now?)
and though a man's mind might endow

even a tree with some excess
of life to which a man seems witness,

that life is not the life of men.
And that is where the joy came in.

Throughout Christian Wiman's work, one senses both presence and absence. It expresses the liminality of hope: hope is there and not there. Its appearance is only possible when you miss something or someone dearly. All we can do is search. The best way out is always through, hoping for the day that poet Wendell Berry mentions in one his 'Sabbath' poems:

There is a day
when the road neither
comes nor goes, and the way
is not a way but a place.

To hear Wiman read his poem 'From a window', scan the QR-code.

REFERENCES AND BIBLIOGRAPHICAL INFORMATION

Major publications:

Poetry

Wiman, C. (2016). *Hammer is the Prayer: Selected Poems.* Macmillan.

Wiman, C. (Ed.). (2021). *Home: 100 Poems.* Yale University Press.

Wiman, C. (Ed.). (2017). *Joy: 100 Poems.* Yale University Press.

Prose and poetry

Wiman, C. (2013). *My Bright Abyss: Meditation of a Modern Believer.* Farrar, Straus and Giroux.

Wiman, C. (2018). *He Held Radical Light: The Art of Faith, the Faith of Art.* Farrar, Straus and Giroux.

Wiman, C. (2023). *Zero at the Bone: Fifty Entries Against Despair.* Farrar, Straus and Giroux.

ABOUT THE AUTHOR

Mark van Vuuren is associate professor of positive organizing at the University of Twente, the Netherlands.

GEORDIN HILL-LEWIS

Cape Town – a city of hope for all

BY JAN JORRIT HASSELAAR AND JULIETA MATOS CASTAÑO

ARTWORK BY JANWILLEM HOFTIJZER

ABSTRACT

This essay examines Geordin Hill-Lewis's view of hope as the driver of long-term urban development grounded in inclusion and expanded opportunity for all. In this vision, hope becomes a shared civic aspiration. Through concrete actions showing that decline is not inevitable, hope emerges as a practical force shaping a city's future and inspiring others.

KEYWORDS

inclusion, civic, community

BIOGRAPHY

Geordin Hill-Lewis (b. 1986) grew up in Cape Town, attending Edgemead High School before going on to study politics, philosophy, and economics at the University of Cape Town. He later obtained a Master's in finance at the University of London, specializing in economic policy. In addition to his public life, he is husband to Carla and father

Hasselaar, Jan Jorrit, Mark van Vuuren, Julieta Matos Castaño, and Erik Borgman, eds. *Voices of Hope: Rediscovering and Building Hope for All.* Amsterdam: Amsterdam University Press / Central European University Press, 2026.
 DOI 10.5117/9789048577347-29

to an eight-year-old daughter – a role that grounds his sense of responsibility for the future.

His interest in politics was awakened at a young age by his schoolteachers who introduced him to books that opened his eyes to the real issues facing South Africa, sparking an interest in the country's history and politics. This early awakening was reinforced in the early 2000s through the weekly newsletters of then President Thabo Mbeki and then leader of the Democratic Alliance, Tony Leon. Through these contrasting and carefully argued perspectives, he came to see that it was possible to change and build the country through careful thought, creativity, and a genuine concern for its people. As a high school student, he became politically active, drawn to the question of how societies can be shaped for the better.

At university, he founded the Democratic Alliance Students' Organization (DASO) based on the conviction that young people needed a stronger voice in the country's democracy. He later served as chief of staff to the premier of Western Cape, Helen Zille, developing a deeper understanding of governance and the importance of institutional integrity.

In 2011, at just 24 years old, he was elected to the National Assembly as the youngest Member of Parliament at the time. Over the next decade, he worked across portfolios including trade, and industry and finance, eventually becoming the Shadow Minister of Finance. These years deepened his understanding of how economic policy and service delivery intersect in shaping people's everyday lives.

On 18 November 2021, Hill-Lewis was inaugurated as the youngest mayor of Cape Town. Stepping into office at a time of widespread national disillusionment, he did so with a clear sense of higher purpose: to restore hope in South Africa by turning Cape Town into living proof that a caring society remains possible.

GEORDIN HILL-LEWIS ON HOPE

When Geordin Hill-Lewis addressed the people of Cape Town for the first time as mayor in 2021, he talked about a powerful idea: to make Cape Town a 'City of Hope for All', especially for the poorest residents. This was the beginning of a purpose-driven journey. Standing before the city, he focused on hope as the essential fuel of any society and warned that no constitutional democracy can survive without it. Hope, he said, is the belief that things can change and that even the most complex problems can be solved through collective effort and good governance.

In his address, Mayor Hill-Lewis was equally clear about the national context: 'The South Africa of 2021 is not the place our parents dreamed of in 1994. Our country is enveloped by a sense of fear and anxiety that things are headed in the wrong direction.' He recognized that more and more South Africans were feeling hopeless about the future. Years of corruption and unmet commitments have eroded public trust and left many citizens with the feeling that the future was narrowing rather than opening up. Hill-Lewis acknowledged that words alone are no longer enough and that it was time for fresh and different thinking.

His response has been to insist on a different standard of leadership. From the outset, he has committed his administration to what he calls 'a higher purpose': restoring hope in South Africa by turning Cape Town into living proof that poverty can be reduced, that the shadows of the past can be confronted, and a more caring society remains possible. Cape Town, he said, must become 'a beacon of hope for South Africa at a time when millions of [...] citizens believe that our country is past the point of no return and where local governments can do nothing more than manage decline'.

Beyond policies and programmes, Mayor Hill-Lewis has always emphasized that hope must be felt in the lived experience of the citizens of Cape Town. Hope is connected to dignity, and it begins with the basics: reliable services, safe communities, and access to opportunity. He argued that it is impossible to speak credibly about hope while residents live with overflowing sewers, broken infrastructure, or unanswered service complaints. Restoring dignity requires attention to these fundamentals, delivered with respect to everyone regardless of where they live in the city. What some may take for granted can, for others, mark the difference between merely *surviving* and *truly living*.

The city's commitment to basic infrastructure has become an essential response. By accelerating the replacement of ageing sewer pipes and setting ambitious targets, Cape Town has treated sanitation as a matter of dignity. For residents affected by repeated sewer spills, these interventions can be life-changing, restoring a sense of care to everyday life. This emphasis is echoed in the city's water strategy, which recognizes that access to water and sanitation is fundamental to citizens' quality of life. The strategy prioritizes improvements for residents in informal settlements.

Another example is the expansion of the MyCiTi Bus service into the city's south-east, extending affordable, reliable, and safe public transport to areas such as Khayelitsha and Mitchells Plain. By linking residents more directly to economic hubs, this initiative helps to undo long-standing spatial inequalities. Hill-Lewis sees safe and reliable public transport as essential to restoring hope by connecting people to what the city has to offer.

Work is at the heart of Hill-Lewis's vision of hope. Employment, he believes, brings purpose in a way that nothing else can because it allows people to shape their own destinies and, very importantly, provide for their families. Economic growth, in this view, is the most sustainable path out of poverty and dependence. As he states in his inaugural address, nothing provides a sense of dignity and pride like employment.

Hope, however, cannot be delivered by the government alone. Hill-Lewis has emphasized the role of active citizens and community organizations in caring for shared spaces and building the city together. Within this framing, good governance becomes a moral obligation. Transparency, accountability, and integrity are non-negotiable pillars of a City of Hope for All, particularly in a context where corruption has long harmed the most vulnerable citizens.

Hill-Lewis also places emphasis on imagination paired with action, because restoring hope requires the courage to envision a future that is better than the present: a city with reliable and sustainable energy, integrated public transport, safer communities, affordable housing, and thriving local businesses. However, imagination must be matched by action. At the close of his inaugural address, he challenged Capetonians: 'We must also rediscover the courage to envision the future that we want. I invite you to join me in imagining a Cape Town with reliable, sustainable, and affordable electricity for all [...] now let's stop imagining this future and let's start building it.'

In his Mayoral Minute (2025), the century-old tradition of an end-of-year message by the mayor of Cape Town, Hill-Lewis presented a series of meaningful steps towards building a City of Hope for All, including significant improvements in infrastructure, housing, and employment. Nevertheless, the mayor concludes by stating that building a city of hope is not a quick task but a journey that will shape Cape Town for decades to come.

Ultimately, Cape Town as a City of Hope for All is about showing that decline is not inevitable, and that through shared responsibility and sustained effort, a different trajectory is possible. Hill-Lewis often comes back to an inspiring belief: that South Africa's best days are ahead of us. By placing hope at the centre of governance, Cape Town is rebuilding trust in a future that can still be shaped together.

REFERENCES AND BIBLIOGRAPHICAL INFORMATION

Our Shared Water Future: Cape Town's Water Strategy (2019). Available at: Cape Town Water Strategy.pdf

Inaugural speech of Mayor Hill-Lewis (2021): A City of Hope.

Cape Town Mayoral Minute 2025 from Mayor Geordin Hill-Lewis: capetown.gov.za/Media-and-news/An end of year note from Mayor Geordin Hill-Lewis

ABOUT THE AUTHORS

Jan Jorrit Hasselaar, economist and theologian, is associate professor of public theology and director of the Amsterdam Centre for Religion & Sustainable Development at Vrije Universiteit Amsterdam, the Netherlands. He is a research fellow at the University of the Free State, South Africa. Jan Jorrit is co-chair of the Global Network for Public Theology.

Julieta Matos Castaño is a research associate at Vrije Universiteit Amsterdam and a practitioner in the field of futures thinking and design at Futures Compass, based in the Netherlands.

MALALA YOUSAFZAI

Hope in education for all

BY JACOB BOUWMAN

ARTWORK BY JANWILLEM HOFTIJZER

ABSTRACT

This essay explores Malala Yousafzai's conviction that education is the foundation of hope. Learning opens pathways to equality and social transformation. Her advocacy demonstrates how the right to education becomes a global expression of hope for every person.

KEYWORDS

education, equality, voice

BIOGRAPHY

The question 'Who is Malala?' carries a bitter taste. It was the question asked by the gunman who stormed the school bus on 12 October 2012. Malala (b. 1997) was on her way back from the school that her father had founded for girls in Mingora, a city in Pakistan's Swat Valley. Most of her classmates wanted to become doctors. But outside the school walls, what prevailed was the Taliban's ideology which forbid girls from going to school. Malala could not understand why

Hasselaar, Jan Jorrit, Mark van Vuuren, Julieta Matos Castaño, and Erik Borgman, eds. *Voices of Hope: Rediscovering and Building Hope for All.* Amsterdam: Amsterdam University Press / Central European University Press, 2026.
 DOI 10.5117/9789048577347-30

educated women, especially doctors, were seen as a threat. She comforted herself with the thought that the Taliban had never killed a girl, but that morning, events nearly proved her wrong. She survived the attack against her and, in her biography 'I am Malala,' she provides the answer to this treacherous question.

Malala Yousafzai describes her childhood as warm and rooted in the traditions of a Pashtun family. She was aware of the cultural expectations placed on girls in Afghanistan and describes how her mother found it difficult to tell her husband that she had given birth to a daughter. The family held education – learning and teaching alike – as their highest ideal. Her father succeeded in establishing a school for girls, and her mother regretted leaving school too soon.

In 2009, when the Taliban came to power, Malala was forced to say goodbye to her class and flee Mingora together with her family. From the beginning of that year, she had been blogging under the pseudonym Gul Makai for BBC Urdu, writing about the increasingly restricted lives of girls under Taliban rule. From mid-January, going to school was banned altogether.

Experiencing this fearful and horrible time, she talked about her nightmares and her fear of being exposed as a blogger. Once, a passerby shouted 'I'll kill you' into his phone, and she panicked, thinking the words were meant for her. She recognized her own sadness in Anne Frank's diary. However, she refused to be intimidated and decided to wear a pink dress even when she was advised not to wear brightly coloured clothing.

She was overjoyed when her family was able to return to Mingora and she found her bag of schoolbooks intact. 'One child, one teacher, one book, and one pen can change the world' became her mantra. Even the 2012 attack did not stop her from demanding education for girls. After she was shot, the family moved to England for reconstructive surgery and her safety. Recognition soon followed in the form of international awards. In 2014, at the age of 17, she became the youngest-ever recipient of the Nobel Peace Prize. She started studying philosophy, politics, and economics at Oxford University. Together with her father, she founded the Malala Fund, which aims to ensure that the 122 million girls worldwide who are still denied education can finally go to school.

MALALA YOUSAFZAI ON HOPE

Malala does not give theoretical lectures on the theme of hope. In her speech at the United Nations, she says that weakness, fear, and hopelessness died the moment she was shot, and that strength, power, and courage were born in her to stand up for the right to education for everyone, including girls. For Malala, going to school is a basic necessity. Her bravery in defending this need makes her a symbol of hope for many.

This view of education as foundational mirrors the American psychologist Abraham Maslow's hierarchy of human needs, which is often depicted as a pyramid. In this model, education is linked to the top three levels of the pyramid. The first basic needs are physiological, such as the need for food, drink, and sleep. It is only when these layers are secure that the needs for love and belonging arise, followed by the need for recognition. Once all these needs are fulfilled, self-actualization can become an urgent and important need. Education is linked to connection, recognition, and self-actualization.

If the Maslow hierarchy implies that people must first wait for the lower levels to be fulfilled before pursuing education, then Malala strongly disagrees. In her speeches, she certainly advocates for the bottom two layers: peace and basic security. However, she insists that we should not wait for these to be realized, because education is precisely a driver to give these two a chance. In her view, education lays the foundation for almost all the needs in the pyramid. It is clearly much more than a composite need from the top three layers. For Malala, education becomes practically synonymous with hope.

This perspective raises one of her central questions: why would the Taliban oppose women's education? The Quran, she points out, actually asks people, including women, to develop their talents. However, the Taliban portray Allah as a rigidly conservative being who, they claim, wishes to prevent the development of half the world's population. Malala believes that opponents of education for girls and women are afraid of the changes in society that result from women gaining knowledge.

As she describes in her biography, Malala was born into a patriarchal society where having a son was clearly preferred. Her mother even hesitated to tell her father that she had given birth to a daughter, fearing his reaction. Fortunately, her father was a feminist who, from the moment he looked into Malala's eyes, made no distinction between his daughters and his sons.

In a patriarchal society, the distinction between men and women functions as a foundational ordering principle. This distinction is not just about power or biological differences. It becomes a vessel for projecting variations, creating rigid identities that shape social debate. Within this logic of identity and difference, deviations from the norm are treated as threatening and strange. This justifies different, often worse treatment, even in matters where this dichotomy is of little relevance. A notorious example is the Greek philosopher Aristotle's definition of woman: he claimed a woman is a man with a deficiency, namely a lack of reason. As a result, the logical conclusion seems to be that education and study are not meaningful for women. Such conclusions arise not from reality itself but from the conceptual categories through which reality is interpreted.

Malala challenges this entire framework not through abstract argument but through practical action. Instead of debating categories and logic, she works with the Malala Fund to ensure that all women receive twelve years of education. For her, hope is a practice that involves a child, a teacher, a book, and a pen!

REFERENCES AND BIBLIOGRAPHICAL INFORMATION

Yousafzai, M., & Lamb, C. (2013). *I am Malala: The Girl who Stood up for Education and was Shot by the Taliban*. Weidenfeld & Nicolson.

Malala Fund. (n.d.). *Malala Fund.* https://malala.org/

ABOUT THE AUTHOR

Jacob Bouwman is a philosopher and programme developer in the Department of University Relations and Fundraising at Vrije Universiteit Amsterdam, the Netherlands.

AMANDA GORMAN

Believing beyond disaster

BY ERIK BORGMAN
ARTWORK BY JANWILLEM HOFTIJZER

ABSTRACT
This essay explores how Amanda Gorman's work connects us through hope to people whose histories have been broken and whose lives bear damage, as well as to a wounded earth and universe. Her poetry links human experience and nature, recognizing that marginalized communities must make extraordinary efforts to realize their full potential.

KEYWORDS
healing, interconnection, resilience

BIOGRAPHY

Amanda Gorman (b. 1998) was only 22 years old when she became world famous for her performance during the inauguration of Joe Biden as the 46th president of the United States of America on 20 January 2020. Yet this Black poet and spoken word artist had already distinguished herself long before that moment. In 2015, when she was just 16, she published her first collection of poems entitled *The*

Hasselaar, Jan Jorrit, Mark van Vuuren, Julieta Matos Castaño, and Erik Borgman, eds. *Voices of Hope: Rediscovering and Building Hope for All.* Amsterdam: Amsterdam University Press / Central European University Press, 2026.
 DOI 10.5117/9789048577347-31

One for Whom Food Is Not Enough. In 2017, at the age of 19, she was elected the first National Youth Poet Laureate of the United States. In the course of 2020, she graduated with honours from the prestigious Harvard University. It may seem like a life full of successes. But as a child, Amanda Gorman struggled with a challenging speech impediment. Like many Black children, she was also raised by a single mother. Gorman considers herself not only a writer but also an activist. She fights for the rights and dignity of Blacks and women, and against climate change. 'It's not enough for me to write,' she said in an interview in 2018, 'I have to do right as well.' Amanda Gordon is a Black Catholic. She belongs to St. Brigid Catholic Church in Los Angeles, a parish entrusted to the Josephites. Since the American Civil War, this religious community has focused specifically on pastoral care for African Americans.

Against the backdrop of the violence with which the US Capitol was stormed two weeks earlier by supporters of Donald Trump, and with the racist slogans that were carried and chanted during the event fresh in mind, Gorman did not just speak about the courage to be the light that the gospel says should be put on a candlestick so that everyone in the house can see it (Luke 8:16; cf. Matthew 5:15; Mark 4:21) – she *displayed* courage. Gorman said she was terrified of what could happen to her in Washington. At the same time, she was convinced that her fear was a sign of the importance of her actions. The space of the Capitol 'needed to be revisited; that space needed to be revamped, and it needed to be reconciled with,' she felt.

AMANDA GORMAN ON HOPE

Both Catholic and Black traditions resonate in the poem that Gorman recited at Biden's inauguration, entitled 'The Hill We Climb'. The poem is particularly impressive because of its combination of militancy and the realization that members of disadvantaged groups must make extraordinary efforts to realize their full potential. But miraculously, the potential tends to unfold. Many people were particularly moved by the ending of the poem:

> Our people diverse and dutiful.
> We will emerge battered but beautiful.
>
> When day comes, we step out of our shades,
> Aflame and unafraid
> The new dawn blooms as we free it.
> For there is always light.
> If only we're brave enough to see it,
> If only we're brave enough to be it.

During the Covid pandemic of 2020 and 2021, Gorman wrote a remarkable collection of poetry entitled *Call Us What We Carry*. It includes the inauguration poem, but otherwise the book contains almost exclusively new writing. The texts connect the militant commitment to the dignity of refugees and Americans of colour with the feeling of stagnation and isolation during the lockdown – which hit Black Americans much harder than other population groups in the United States – and with a remarkable attention to nature and the precarious situation in which it finds itself. Here Gorman shows herself sensitive to the fact that 'nature poetry' easily evokes an image of, as she puts it, 'old white men on benches thinking about existentialism' – in her view 'completely removed and isolated from any kind of real profound question about race, equality ... life'. For her part, she purposely tries to connect poetry about nature with such questions 'from the perception of the marginalized, who typically are the people who are tending the earth, who are [planting] the crops, who are being removed from the land'. The result is a hopeful reconnection between people whose histories have been broken and lives damaged, and the wounded earth they inhabit.

But, Amanda Gorman warns, 'Hope is no silent harbour, no haven still. / it is the roaring thing that tugs us away / From the very shores we clutch'. In a poem whose title – 'What We Carry' – suggests that it is meant to clarify the title of her collection, Gorman observes:

> We have learned our true names —
> Not what we are called
> But what we are called to carry forth from here
> What do we carry, if not
> What & who we care most for ...

To clarify 'what & who we care most for', Gorman presents nature as precarious, messy, and at the same time wondrous – just as the existence of people in the margins is precarious, messy, and at the same time wondrous. She writes:

> As kids we sat in grass,
> Fished our hands into the dirt.
> We felt the damp brown
> Universe writhe, alert & alive,
> Earth cupped in the boat of our hands.
>
> Our eyes waxed with wonder.
> Children understand:
> Even grime is a gift,
> Even what is mired is miraculous,
> What is marred is still marvellous.

The 'boat of our hands' suggests Noah's Ark, and the open hands forming the boat are elsewhere in the poem described as 'a blooming thing'. It is the bloom of love, of which Gorman says that it brings loss – 'Loss is the cost of loving' – but this loss is at the same time the treasure. It connects people with the damaged earth, the mired universe that demands our concern yet still has the power to fascinate and move us – because, despite everything, it carries us.

This love – impressed, fascinated, and painful – Gorman treasures in the words she writes, fully aware of the importance of her task:

Words matter, for
Language is an ark. [...]
Language is a life craft,
Yes,
Language is a life raft.

So that the earth – alert and alive but marred – is not lost but reveals its damaged, true beauty, Gorman phrases it as 'One globe, wonder-flawed'. In her poetry, Gorman toasts 'to the preservation / Of a light so terrific'. Everything ultimately comes down to dedication to this light: 'What are we, / If not the price of light', she asks – 'the price' here meaning both what must be paid and the emblem of victory. In Gorman's vision, we pay with our lives for the light we carry and spread, and at the same time, life is what we receive along the way. In a surprising way, the Gospel adage that those who lose their lives will gain them is made concrete here.

Gorman sees people whose lives have been damaged and sullied and who have a hidden beauty in precisely that, as bearers of the light of the world. We 'believe beyond disaster,' she concludes. This Gorman presents as the deepest identity and dignity of human beings. This is what the title of her poetry collection ultimately indicates:

... what we have left
Is all we need.
We are enough,
Armed only
With our hands,
Open but unemptied,
Just like a blooming thing.
We walk into tomorrow,
Carrying nothing
But the world.

REFERENCES AND BIBLIOGRAPHICAL INFORMATION

Gorman, A. (n.d.). *Amanda Gorman.* https://www.theamandagorman.com/

Gorman, A. (2022). *Call Us What We Carry.* Vintage.

Smith, C. (2021, December 16). 'I Always Think of Poetry as Home for Me.' *The Atlantic.* https://www.theatlantic.com/ideas/archive/2021/12/amanda-gorman-poetry-call-us-what-we-carry/621019/

Walsh, C. (2018, October 4). 'The Poetic Perspective.' *The Harvard Gazette.* https://news.harvard.edu/gazette/story/2018/10/youth-poet-laureate-amanda-gorman-delivers-poem-at-harvard-presidents-inauguration/

ABOUT THE AUTHOR

Erik Borgman is a lay Dominican and professor emeritus of public theology at Tilburg University, the Netherlands.

YAHYA MAHMMOUD

Hope is in creating hopeful memories

BY ERIK BORGMAN

ARTWORK BY JANWILLEM HOFTIJZER

ABSTRACT

This essay explores Yahya Mahmoud's example of how hope can be created even in places marked by devastation. By crafting 'hopeful memories' and sharing small acts of care and normalcy from the ruins of Gaza, he creates meaning for himself and others. His gestures become acts of resistance that help hope to take hold and grow.

KEYWORDS

memory, dignity, care

BIOGRAPHY

He could easily have remained unknown if the devastating war in Gaza had not taken place. A young man of 22 in Gaza, studying pharmacy and dubbing advertising videos to earn some money. But the war did take place, and Yahya Mahmmoud has thousands of followers who know that he built a studio in a closet amid the rubble of his house to tell the stories of what is happening to him and the people around him, distributing the recordings via social media. He

---

Hasselaar, Jan Jorrit, Mark van Vuuren, Julieta Matos Castaño, and Erik Borgman, eds. *Voices of Hope: Rediscovering and Building Hope for All.* Amsterdam: Amsterdam University Press / Central European University Press, 2026.
 DOI 10.5117/9789048577347-32

is determined to remain visible and audible, not to be swept away and buried in the rubble. He makes no secret of the extreme difficulty of the situation. Hardly any buildings are left undamaged, there is a shortage of everything, and Gazans are perpetually forced to seek refuge elsewhere. It is no longer safe where they live, and where they are supposed to go it will not be any safer. Like his comrades in fate, he has no possibility of escape. But he does not want to suffer passively. He wants to tell his own story in his own words, refusing to become a mere statistic. It is the only freedom he has under the circumstances, and he clings to it with everything he has.

Yahya sticks to his own standards. War or no war, the sound of his recordings must be clean and clear. He has done everything he can to ensure the quality of his audio clips – egg cartons on the walls of the closet to dampen the echo, a sock over the microphone of his cell phone to make the sound less sharp. He wants to write down his texts before he reads them out, but pen and paper have become almost unaffordable in Gaza. He may need to walk for hours to find them. 'So sometimes I use one sheet of paper for a month,' he says, 'and write on it in very small handwriting.' Finding places with electricity to charge his equipment is challenging. Several times he narrowly escaped death because he was in places with internet access.

Those around him have advised him to stop doing what he is doing and limit himself to what young men are supposed to do during wartime: securing water and food, helping their families. But he believes that what he is doing serves a higher purpose. It helps not only him but also others not to lose their sense of humanity.

YAHYA MAHMMOUD ON HOPE

After a year of war in Gaza, Yahya Mahmmoud saw that people were losing all hope because of what was happening. He was convinced that this was highly dangerous, as it would kill their will to live. He came up with the idea of creating 99 hopeful memories to counterbalance all the misery, writing these memories down and putting the notes in a jar. He records everything with his cell phone and shares the videos on his Instagram account. In one of them, we see Yahya clearing one wall of a house that has been shot to pieces, carefully painting it white, and writing on it, in Arabic and English: 'All we dream is to live in peace.'

Another video shows him reading to a few children who have not been able to go to school for a long time and teaching them how to write. It makes them visibly happy. He carefully sets up a place where he and a friend can watch a soccer game together on his laptop – a fragment of normality amidst the overwhelming violence. The video that shows him putting his textbooks in an old refrigerator he found somewhere among the rubble is particularly moving. He first cleans it carefully. He cannot use his books now, with all educational institutions closed, so he stores them there as a symbolic safeguard for the future – for the day he can resume his education. It is a quiet gesture of hope.

Still another video shows Yahya reading letters sent to him — miraculously, there is still mail in Gaza from time to time. Yahya is visibly touched that his videos have been comforting to others. From one of the envelopes falls a tasbih, the prayer beads that Muslims use to recite the Ninety-Nine Beautiful Names of God: the Merciful, the Compassionate, the Holy, the Peaceful, the Creator, the Almighty, the All-Knowing, the Giver of Faith, the Unifier, the Exalter, and so on. The 99 videos that Yahya Mahmmoud wants to make can indeed be considered tributes to God's holy names. Ultimately, they all refer to that one name that is unspeakable and known only to God himself.

Yahya Mahmmoud's recordings together form a true work of art. As befits a good piece of art, his videos open up the world in a new way, making it visible as a place full of hopeful gestures and signs that, despite everything, testify to confidence in the future. 'With these memories, I address every person on earth,' says Yahya. He feels certain that his message will be heard because it is directed at everything that is human, regardless of anything else.

In this way, he also keeps his own hope alive with his videos. At the end of 2024, he said in an interview:

> Today, I am more determined than ever not to leave my country until the war is over. Whether we live or die, I am sure that hope will always remain and that life will return to this beautiful place. I hope with all my heart that the 99 memories will all be complete and that I can put them in a book that will be translated into many languages.

He concludes:

> Maybe I can enter this idea in an international competition when the war is over... Oh, God! Or when there is a ceasefire... Oh God! The news of the ceasefire would be the best news ever!

With a six-week ceasefire began on 19 January 2025, Yahya organized a children's version of the talent show Arabs Got Talent. He claimed that going through all the experiences of war, Arab kids have developed a unique talent to survive in a joyful manner under devastating circumstances. The video shows the kids happily celebrating the possibility to freely sing, dance, and juggle.

Although the ceasefire was intended to be a first step toward lasting peace, after the six-week period had passed, the fighting resumed. And during the next ceasefire, it never fully stopped. In the winter of 2025 –26, Yahya has reported how he and his neighbours are struggling to cope with the cold.

REFERENCES AND BIBLIOGRAPHICAL INFORMATION

Yahya Mahmmoud's Instagram account is here: www.instagram.com/yahya_mahmmoud/

Yahya Mahmmoud was interviewed for the Dutch newspaper *Trouw*. The interview was published on 14 December 2024.

ABOUT THE AUTHOR

Erik Borgman is a lay Dominican and professor emeritus of public theology at Tilburg University, the Netherlands.

AUTUMN PELTIER

Hope carried through water

BY MARK VAN VUUREN

ARTWORK BY JANWILLEM HOFTIJZER

ABSTRACT

This essay explores Autumn Peltier's understanding of hope through water as a source of life and a bond across generations. For Peltier, grief and anger are honest beginnings; without them, hope grows thin. When grief is honoured, it fuels change, deepens stewardship, and opens space for many voices, creating a choir that cannot be ignored.

KEYWORDS

water, intergeneration, stewardship

BIOGRAPHY

Autumn Peltier (b. 2004) is an activist and advocate for Indigenous communities across Canada. She is of Anishinaabe heritage, more specifically the Ojibwe tribe. Their homeland, Ojibwewaki, covers part of what is now Canada and the US, including the Great Lakes region and the Northern Plains, extending into the subarctic and throughout the northeastern woodlands. Inspired by her aunt Jose-

---

Hasselaar, Jan Jorrit, Mark van Vuuren, Julieta Matos Castaño, and Erik Borgman, eds. *Voices of Hope: Rediscovering and Building Hope for All.* Amsterdam: Amsterdam University Press / Central European University Press, 2026.

 DOI 10.5117/9789048577347-33

phine Mandamin, who was a well-known 'water walker', Autumn's activism started at a very young age. A 'water walker' is a woman who has walked around all five of the Great Lakes to raise awareness about water protection.

At the age of 13, Autumn was chosen to give the Canadian prime minister Trudeau a gift: a water bundle (a sacred bundle of objects). While giving the gift, she told the prime minister: 'I am very unhappy with the choices you have made.' According to the indigenous peoples, the government failed to provide their communities with clean drinking water, threatening the water supply through leaking pipelines. She succeeded her great-grandmother as Chief Water Commissioner for the Anishinabek Nation, representing 39 First Nations communities. Before turning 15, Autumn Peltier became a regular speaker at the United Nations Secretary-General's Climate Action Summits. An honorary doctorate was awarded to her while she was still in the 12th grade. She continues to receive many recognitions and awards by people and institutes who mostly keep on refusing to honour her wishes.

AUTUMN PELTIER ON HOPE

She is clear about the priorities: 'We can't eat money or drink oil.' She knows the cause: 'We're realizing what kind of future the adults today are giving us for tomorrow.' For this reason, Autumn speaks up to tell the adults to change their priorities. Watching the documentary 'The Water Walker' is a sobering experience. The message is so simple: there is no life without water, so acknowledge the water as a spiritual gift. Caring for water (and for all of nature) is an act of hope for current and future generations.

Autumn Peltier is so *young*. The moment she starts crying in the documentary is when she tells how she was bullied by her classmates 'because not a lot of kids get to do the stuff I was doing like meeting the prime minister'. It is not the great threats and wicked problems that made her tear up at that moment but the rejection from her classmates. It reminds the viewers that she is still a child.

At the same time, Autumn Peltier is so *old*. She drinks from a deep and ancient well. Autumn speaks often about her ancestors and how she imagines herself already as an ancestor. She has a broad view not just on matters of concern but also in terms of time. It is impressive how she has the ability to turn anger and injustice into action, youth into leadership, and care for water into a vision of a better future.

With water as the source of her caring, Autumn Peltier advocates for a range of entities – first and foremost, water itself. In Anishinaabe tradition, water is considered a living spirit. It is treated with respect because it sustains all forms of life and is seen as a gift from the Creator. 'Water is life' is a phrase she uses frequently because clean water is essential to the health and survival of people, animals, plants, and ecosystems. For her, protecting water is equivalent to protecting life itself. By doing this, she gives voice to nature in general, and water in particular.

Flowing out of her concern for water is her commitment to women. In many Anishinaabe communities, women hold the responsibility of being 'water carriers'. This means they have a sacred duty to care for and protect water. Third, she advocates for future generations. Autumn emphasizes that water protection is not only a spiritual duty but also a generational responsibility. She views water as sacred because future generations depend on it, and harming water harms the world they will inherit. And fourth, her advocacy gives a voice to indigenous people. Autumn Peltier's advocacy is deeply connected to Indigenous people because it grows directly out of Indigenous teachings, responsibilities, and lived experiences. Her work comes from Indigenous identity, culture, and rights. Many Indigenous communities in Canada have faced decades-long boil-water advisories because their water sources were contaminated. They suffer from inadequate or failing water systems, lack of government action, and industrial pollution in their reserves.

Autumn's actions connect to hope in different ways. It shows the importance of grief and anger as a starting point. One cannot overestimate the low point that serves as a starting point for her advocacy. Without grief, hope can become cheap. And when held honestly, grief has the ability to fuel hope and make change possible.

The roles given to her create a platform through which she can be heard. She gives voice to the voiceless. Speaking on behalf of others is powerful, as she includes so many others: water, nature, women, indigenous people, and future generations. Bringing all these voices together creates a choir that is hard to ignore.

The simplicity of her actions ('I am very unhappy with the choices you have made') echo the simple school strike with which Greta Thunberg unexpectedly ignited a global movement. Sometimes it is the simple actions, motivated by grief and anger, that lead to the biggest consequences.

REFERENCES AND BIBLIOGRAPHICAL INFORMATION

Lindstrom, C. (2023). *Autumn Peltier, Water Warrior.* Roaring Brook Press.

Documentary: The Water Walker. https://www.weareseeingred.com/film

ABOUT THE AUTHOR

Mark van Vuuren is associate professor of positive organizing at the University of Twente, the Netherlands.

Can we be surprised by hope once more?

Across the voices we have gathered in this collection, a few things stand out. First of all, it is clear what hope is *not*. Hope is not the same as optimism. It is not about believing that tomorrow will be better than today. Hope is also not merely an emotion or a feeling.

Crucially, hope means living in tension, *directed toward what is not yet, without denying what already is*. Many voices vouch for that, from Thomas Aquinas to Reinhold Niebuhr and Václav Havel, and from Jürgen Moltmann to Charles Snyder and John Caputo. Hope in this sense is an orientation of heart and spirit; something we practice because it is good in itself, without knowing what the outcome will be.

A life lived in hope is shaped by *the conviction that the world is often not the way it should be, and that none of us should reconcile ourselves to that fact*. Among others, Frederick Douglass, Martin Luther King Jr., Nelson Mandela, Desmond Tutu, Martha Nussbaum, and Allan Boesak show us hope as a kind of moral strength, inviting us to refuse to accept injustice and oppression as the final word. People like King and Tutu show us that hope is a discipline. Seen that way, hope becomes a form of resistance, guided by a sense of love and justice that refuses despair and violence as responses.

Hasselaar, Jan Jorrit, Mark van Vuuren, Julieta Matos Castaño, and Erik Borgman, eds. *Voices of Hope: Rediscovering and Building Hope for All.* Amsterdam: Amsterdam University Press / Central European University Press, 2026.
 DOI 10.5117/9789048577347-34

Thus, hope does not exist apart from suffering. Etty Hillesum, Viktor Frankl, and Johann Baptist Metz show us that hope is learning *to live within pain and tragedy* and is often mixed with melancholy, loss, and disappointment. And even then, it keeps moving, pausing when it needs to, then rising again.

A central resource that keeps hope alive is relationship formed along the way. Jonathan Sacks, Archbishop Thabo Makgoba, Russell Botman, and Pope Francis all emphasize that hope is not an event but rather *a journey that must be practiced together*. It grows through small and courageous steps, reconciliation, forgiveness, shared responsibility, and the rebuilding of trust. It takes shape in institutions, (religious) communities, universities, and movements that dare to remain open to one another, even when history or the world divides them.

This communal side of hope shows up in civic and social leadership. Voices such as Malala Yousafzai, Pope Leo XIV, Imtiaz Sooliman, Geordin Hill-Lewis, and Frits Goldschmeding remind us that hope is public, too, and *practiced through concrete acts of care and service* in society and the economy. Hope becomes real when it is translated into responsibility for the common good.

Hope calls for imagination as well. Without the ability to imagine alternatives, it collapses into resignation. Audre Lorde, Paul Ricoeur, Christian Wiman, Amanda Gorman, and Yahya Mahmoud show us that imagination is a way of widening reality. Even in the face of seemingly insurmountable challenges and the recognition of our inadequacies, *hope continues to imagine what might be*, drawing us into a habitual movement towards the good (in Aquinas's sense). Poetic, narrative, artistic, and philosophical forms of expression can keep hope alive when systems fail and the future feels closed off.

People like Jane Goodall, Autumn Peltier, and the Ecumenical Patriarch Bartholomew widen the frame of hope beyond the human. They inspire us to recognize that *our relationship with nature* fosters hope: caring for the earth, the earth caring for us, respecting life, and taking responsibility for future generations.

Across generations, from Thomas Aquinas to Etty Hillesum, from Desmond Tutu to the youngest voices we have gathered in this collection, we see hope as a journey carried by pilgrims open to whatever the path offers, supporting one another in the belief that things can become better. In working together, we have rediscovered how much our different roots matter and how we can enrich each other when we really take the time to listen.

The late Pope Francis often spoke of hope as a humble seed, hidden in the soil, slowly growing into a tree. Its many roots are varied, its trunk is shared, and its fruits appear in the everyday practices of justice, reconciliation, joy, imagination, and care that are already taking shape in the world.

Can we be surprised by hope once more? Can we be surprised by hope in a world strained by inequality, social tensions, wars, antidemocratic movements, climate change, biodiversity loss, and the weight of colonial history?

The voices in this collection suggest that we can if we are courageous enough to take that first step and are willing to walk together, build institutions that sustain and protect one another, and allow ourselves to be changed – and surprised – along the way. In the words of one of our youngest Voices of Hope, Amanda Gorman:

> For there is always light,
> if only we're brave enough to see it
> If only we're brave enough to be it

ABOUT THE AUTHORS

Jan Jorrit Hasselaar, economist and theologian, is associate professor of public theology and director of the Amsterdam Centre for Religion & Sustainable Development at Vrije Universiteit Amsterdam, the Netherlands. He is a research fellow at the University of the Free State, South Africa. Jan Jorrit is co-chair of the Global Network for Public Theology.

Mark van Vuuren is associate professor of positive organizing at the University of Twente, the Netherlands.
Julieta Matos Castaño is a research associate at Vrije Universiteit Amsterdam and a practitioner in the field of futures thinking and design at Futures Compass, based in the Netherlands.
Erik Borgman is a lay Dominican and professor emeritus of public theology at Tilburg University, the Netherlands.

List of contributors and editors

Daniël Andrew is lecturer in the Department of Practical and Missional Theology at the University of the Free State, South Africa.

Ernst Bohlmeijer is professor of mental health promotion at the University of Twente, the Netherlands.

Erik Borgman is a lay Dominican and professor emeritus of public theology at Tilburg University, the Netherlands.

Andries Bouwman is mayor of Opsterland, a rural municipality in the north of the Netherlands.

Jacob Bouwman is a philosopher and programme developer in the Department of University Relations and Fundraising at Vrije Universiteit Amsterdam, the Netherlands.

Govert Buijs is a political philosopher and holds the Frits Goldschmeding Chair for Societal and Economic Renewal at Vrije Universiteit Amsterdam, the Netherlands.

Sylvia van de Bunt is the UNESCO Chairholder in Cross-Cultural Sustainability and associate professor at the School of Business and Economics, Vrije Universiteit Amsterdam, the Netherlands.

John Chryssavgis is archdeacon of the Ecumenical Patriarchate and executive director of the Huffington Ecumenical Institute at Hellenic College Holy Cross, the United States.

Miriam Feldmann-Kaye is assistant professor in the Department of Jewish Philosophy at Bar Ilan University, Israel.

Eugene Fortein is senior lecturer in church history and church polity at the Faculty of Theology and Religion, University of the Free State, South Africa.

Jan Jorrit Hasselaar, economist and theologian, is associate professor of public theology and director of the Amsterdam Centre for Religion & Sustainable Development at Vrije Universiteit Amsterdam, the Netherlands. He is a research fellow at the University of the Free

State, South Africa. Jan Jorrit is co-chair of the Global Network for Public Theology.

JanWillem Hoftijzer is a conceptual designer and illustrator at The Sketching Factory and assistant professor and course manager of design sketching and visualization at Delft University of Technology, the Netherlands.

Abigail Hopley is personal assistant and acting chaplain to Archbishop Thabo Makgoba and priest at Good Shepherd Protea, Kirstenbosch, in the Anglican Church of Southern Africa, South Africa.

John Klaasen is dean of the Faculty of Theology and Religion at the University of the Free State, South Africa.

Marius Louw is minister at the English Reformed Church in Amsterdam and a PhD candidate at Stellenbosch University, South Africa and Vrije Universiteit Amsterdam, the Netherlands.

Julieta Matos Castaño is a research associate at Vrije Universiteit Amsterdam and a practitioner in the field of futures thinking and design at Futures Compass, based in the Netherlands.

Trineke Palm is director of the think tank of the ChristenUnie, a Dutch Christian-social political party.

Mcebisi Pinyana is the bishop of the Diocese of Grahamstown in the Anglican Church of Southern Africa, South Africa.

Demaine Solomons is associate professor of systematic theology and ethics at Stellenbosch University, South Africa.

Calvin D. Ullrich is senior lecturer in interdisciplinary theology and director of the Centre for Interdisciplinary Research in Religion, Community, and Ecologies (CIRRCE) at the University of the Free State, South Africa.

Mark van Vuuren is associate professor of positive organizing at the University of Twente, the Netherlands.

Grant Bradley Walters is the bishop of the Diocese of Port Elizabeth in the Anglican Church of Southern Africa, South Africa.

Henco van der Westhuizen is associate professor in systematic theology at the University of the Free State, South Africa and consultant for the Faith and Order Commission (World Council of Churches).

9789048577347